PRINCE2 PRACTITIONER EXAM PRACTICE QUESTIONS & DUMPS

130+ EXAM PRACTICE QUESTIONS FOR PRINCE2 PRACTITIONER UPDATED 2020

– Volume 2

Presented By: Librito Books

Copyright © 2020 by Librito Books

All rights reserved. No part of this publication may be reproduced, distributed, or transmitted in any form or by any means, including photocopying, recording, or other electronic or mechanical methods, without the prior written permission of the publisher, except in the case of brief quotations embodied in critical reviews and certain other noncommercial uses permitted by copyright law.

First Copy Printed in 2020

About Librito Books:

Librito Books is a publishing house based in US, a platform that is available both online & locally, which unleashes the power of educational content, literary collection, poetry & many other book genres. We make it easy for writers & authors to get their books designed, published, promoted, and sell professionally on worldwide scale with eBook + Print distribution. Librito Books was founded in 2016, and is now distributing books worldwide.

Sections

1. Business Case Theme
2. Organization Theme
3. Quality Theme
4. Plans Theme
5. Risk Theme
6. Change Theme
7. Progress Theme
8. Directing a Project, Controlling a Stage and Managing Product Delivery
9. Managing a Stage Boundary and Closing a Project
10. Starting up and Initiating a Project

Note: Find answers at the end of the book

QUESTION 1

Scenario
Additional Information
During the initiation stage the Project Manager met with the Marketing Director to find out more about the requirements of the promotional calendar and recorded the following notes: There has been a reduction in the order numbers at the MNO Manufacturing due in part to the increased marketing activities of its competitors. 10% of customers have not re-ordered in this financial year and staff morale is poor. A number of skilled staff have left as a result and replacement staff have not been recruited due to the reduced operation. If the project is successful, a recruitment campaign will be required to fill the existing staff vacancies and there may be a requirement for additional staff. Operational costs are likely to increase because skilled staff are expensive and difficult to find.

In financial terms, there were a total of 1,500 orders in the last financial year, each with an average profit of £2k. The Marketing department believes that sending a promotional calendar to our current and prospective customers would increase orders by at least 10% with a minimum of 10 further orders from the list of prospective customers within 12 months from the date of distribution.

The Marketing Director will be funding the project from the business marketing budget. She believes that the effect of a good company image portrayed by a successful calendar would last into a second year. She has forecast the same increase in orders for a second year and predicts that the annual employee satisfaction survey will show a measurable improvement in staff morale.

A number of alternatives were explored, including:
20% discount for all repeat customers - not cost-effective and very short term A promotional calendar as a free Christmas gift - would target current and prospective customers and the benefits would last into a second year A series of television and press advertisements· was too expensive
A direct mail shot to all customers - benefit would be short term Creation of an internet website - would not suit all customers

The calendar is seen as the favored option, as long as the company's competitors do not increase their marketing activity. Whilst the Marketing department wants a very high quality, glossy product, the project management team must be aware of the cost this will incur.
Which 2 statements should be recorded under the Business options heading?

A. Produce a promotional calendar as a free Christmas gift to current and prospective customers.
B. Use a professional photographer to create the photographs for the calendar.
C. Create the photographs for the calendar internally.
D. Outsource the creation of the calendar to a professional marketing company.
E. Do nothing.

Section: Business Case Theme

QUESTION 2
Scenario
Additional Information
During the initiation stage the Project Manager met with the Marketing Director to find out more about the requirements of the promotional calendar and recorded the following notes:
There has been a reduction in the order numbers at the MNO Manufacturing due in part to the increased marketing activities of its competitors. 10% of customers have not re-ordered in this financial year and staff morale is poor. A number of skilled staff have left as a result and replacement staff have not been recruited due to the reduced operation. If the project is successful, a recruitment campaign will be required to fill the existing staff vacancies and there may be a requirement for additional staff. Operational costs are likely to increase because skilled staff are expensive and difficult to find.

In financial terms, there were a total of 1,500 orders in the last financial year, each with an average profit of £2k. The Marketing department believes that sending a promotional calendar to our current and prospective customers would increase orders by at least 10% with a minimum of 10 further orders from the list of prospective customers within 12 months from the date of distribution.

The Marketing Director will be funding the project from the business marketing budget. She believes that the effect of a good company image portrayed by a successful calendar would last into a second year. She has forecast the same increase in orders for a second year and predicts that the annual employee satisfaction survey will show a measurable improvement in staff morale.

A number of alternatives were explored, including:
20% discount for all repeat customers - not cost-effective and very short term
A promotional calendar as a free Christmas gift - would target current and prospective customers and the benefits would last into a second year A series of television and press advertisements· was too expensive
A direct mail shot to all customers - benefit would be short term Creation of an internet website - would not suit all customers

The calendar is seen as the favored option, as long as the company's competitors do not increase their marketing activity. Whilst the Marketing department wants a very high quality, glossy product, the project management team must be aware of the cost this will incur.

Which 2 statements should be recorded under the Expected benefits heading?

A. Increase orders by at least 10% with a minimum of 10 further orders from the list of prospective customers within 12 months.
B. It will be similar to calendars sent out in previous years
C. The Marketing department believes that the benefits of a good company image, as portrayed by a successful calendar, will last into a second year and bring the same increase in orders.
D. The calendar will contain photos of both staff and company products.
E. The Marketing department want a very high quality, glossy product as they believe this will be more appealing to customers.

Section: Business Case Theme

QUESTION 3
Scenario
Additional Information
During the initiation stage the Project Manager met with the Marketing Director to find out more about the requirements of the promotional calendar and recorded the following notes:
There has been a reduction in the order numbers at the MNO Manufacturing due in part to the increased marketing activities of its competitors. 10% of customers have not re-ordered in this financial year and staff morale is poor. A number of skilled staff have left as a result and replacement staff have not been recruited due to the reduced operation. If the project is successful, a recruitment campaign will be required to fill the existing staff vacancies and there may be a requirement for additional staff. Operational costs are likely to increase because skilled staff are expensive and difficult to find.

In financial terms, there were a total of 1,500 orders in the last financial year, each with an average profit of £2k. The Marketing department believes that sending a promotional calendar to our current and prospective customers would increase orders by at least 10% with a minimum of 10 further orders from the list of prospective customers within 12 months from the date of distribution.

The Marketing Director will be funding the project from the business marketing budget. She believes that the effect of a good company image portrayed by a successful calendar would last into a second year. She has forecast the same increase in orders for a second year and predicts that the annual employee satisfaction survey will show a measurable improvement in staff morale.

A number of alternatives were explored, including:
20% discount for all repeat customers - not cost-effective and very short term
A promotional calendar as a free Christmas gift - would target current and prospective customers and the benefits would last into a second year A series of television and press advertisements· was too expensive
A direct mail shot to all customers - benefit would be short term Creation of an internet website - would not suit all customers

The calendar is seen as the favored option, as long as the company's competitors do not increase their marketing activity. Whilst the Marketing department wants a very high quality, glossy product, the project management team must be aware of the cost this will incur.

Which 2 statements should be recorded under the Expected dis-benefits heading?

A. A high quality, glossy product will involve additional costs.
B. Individuals in the engineering team who are not selected to appear in the calendar photographs will become de-motivated.
C. The calendar may not result in the expected 10% increase in orders.
D. Because the Calendar project is a priority for the MNO Manufacturing Company, the delivery of other projects within the Marketing department will be delayed.
E. The calendar may not result in the 10 further orders from the list of prospective customers in 12 months.

Section: Business Case Theme

QUESTION 4
Scenario
Additional Information
During the initiation stage the Project Manager met with the Marketing Director to find out more about the requirements of the promotional calendar and recorded the following notes:
There has been a reduction in the order numbers at the MNO Manufacturing due in part to the increased marketing activities of its competitors. 10% of customers have not re-ordered in this financial year and staff morale is poor. A number of skilled staff have left as a result and replacement staff have not been recruited due to the reduced operation. If the project is successful, a recruitment campaign will be required to fill the existing staff vacancies and there may be a requirement for additional staff. Operational costs are likely to increase because skilled staff are expensive and difficult to find.

In financial terms, there were a total of 1,500 orders in the last financial year, each with an average profit of £2k. The Marketing department believes that sending a promotional calendar to our current and prospective customers would increase orders by at least 10% with a minimum of 10 further orders from the list of prospective customers within 12 months from the date of distribution.

The Marketing Director will be funding the project from the business marketing budget. She believes that the effect of a good company image portrayed by a successful calendar would last into a second year. She has forecast the same increase in orders for a second year and predicts that the annual employee satisfaction survey will show a measurable improvement in staff morale.

A number of alternatives were explored, including:
20% discount for all repeat customers - not cost-effective and very short term
A promotional calendar as a free Christmas gift - would target current and prospective customers and the benefits would last into a second year A series of television and press advertisements· was too expensive
A direct mail shot to all customers - benefit would be short term Creation of an internet website - would not suit all customers

The calendar is seen as the favored option, as long as the company's competitors do not increase their marketing activity. Whilst the Marketing department wants a very high quality, glossy product, the project management team must be aware of the cost this will incur. Which 2 statements should be recorded under the Timescale heading?

A. Benefits will be lost if the project is not completed on time.
B. A recruitment campaign to fill the existing staff vacancies will need to take place in the next 12 months.
C. Additional 10% increase in orders in year two.
D. The prepared calendar pack must be delivered by the first week in December.
E. The print company requires a 2 week notification period of the calendar pack delivery.

Section: Business Case Theme

QUESTION 5
Scenario
Additional Information
During the initiation stage the Project Manager met with the Marketing Director to find out more about the requirements of the promotional calendar and recorded the following notes:
There has been a reduction in the order numbers at the MNO Manufacturing due

in part to the increased marketing activities of its competitors. 10% of customers have not re-ordered in this financial year and staff morale is poor. A number of skilled staff have left as a result and replacement staff have not been recruited due to the reduced operation. If the project is successful, a recruitment campaign will be required to fill the existing staff vacancies and there may be a requirement for additional staff. Operational costs are likely to increase because skilled staff are expensive and difficult to find.

In financial terms, there were a total of 1,500 orders in the last financial year, each with an average profit of £2k. The Marketing department believes that sending a promotional calendar to our current and prospective customers would increase orders by at least 10% with a minimum of 10 further orders from the list of prospective customers within 12 months from the date of distribution.

The Marketing Director will be funding the project from the business marketing budget. She believes that the effect of a good company image portrayed by a successful calendar would last into a second year. She has forecast the same increase in orders for a second year and predicts that the annual employee satisfaction survey will show a measurable improvement in staff morale.

A number of alternatives were explored, including:
20% discount for all repeat customers - not cost-effective and very short term
A promotional calendar as a free Christmas gift - would target current and prospective customers and the benefits would last into a second year A series of television and press advertisements· was too expensive
A direct mail shot to all customers - benefit would be short term Creation of an internet website - would not suit all customers

The calendar is seen as the favored option, as long as the company's competitors do not increase their marketing activity. Whilst the Marketing department wants a very high quality, glossy product, the project management team must be aware of the cost this will incur.

Which 2 statements correctly define a Business Case risk which should be recorded under the Major risks heading?

A. Operational costs will increase as a result of the recruitment campaign.
B. The prepared calendar pack is to be delivered to the printers by the first week in December.
C. If the calendar quality is poor customers will not use it, creating the reverse effect and reducing orders further.
D. If any competitors launch a calendar at the same time this will reduce the impact of the MNO calendar and benefits will be reduced.

E. Staff morale will improve as a result of the promotional calendar.

Section: Business Case Theme

QUESTION 6
Scenario
A central government department, the Ministry of Food Hygiene (MFH), faces increasing pressure to cut costs, better manage suppliers' performance and reduce the confusion caused by inadequate internal controls, outdated standards and outdated technology. External consultants were employed to conduct a feasibility study to identify options to address the problems, and the likely costs and benefits. The following options were considered:

- Do nothing.
- Re-engineer selected business functions. Outsource selected business functions.

The feasibility study concluded that there was a case for outsourcing the MFH Information Technology Division and the Facilities Division (maintenance of buildings and grounds). The recommendations were:

- One service provider should be contracted to provide the services currently provided by the Information Technology Division and the Facilities Division. A 10-year service contract should be agreed with the selected service provider.

The feasibility study developed high-level designs of the current organization, processes, systems and operating models, plus an outline Business Case for the required project. The external consultants also made the following recommendations for the management of the project:

- Use PRINCE2.
- Set up the project with 4 management stages:

Stage 1. Standard PRINCE2 initiation activities.
Stage 2. Create detailed designs (future organization, processes, systems and operating models) and the service level agreement between MFH and the future service provider.
Stage 3. Request and evaluate proposals, select service provider and agree contract.
Stage 4. Transfer equipment and staff, transfer responsibility for service provision and run trial period.

Initial estimates indicated that the project would cost £2.5m and take two years to complete.
MFH senior management agreed that there was a case for outsourcing, and accepted the recommendations as a basis for the project. There is an expected

saving of £20m over 10 years.

The Outsourcing project has completed the Starting up a Project process and is now in the initiation stage. Because of the strategic importance of the project, the MFH Chief Executive Officer has taken the role of Executive. A PRINCE2-experienced Project Manager has been appointed from within MFH. Staff within the business functions being outsourced will work with the external consultants who conducted the feasibility study to define the detailed designs.

Which 2 statements should be recorded under the Reasons heading?

A. The lack of up-to-date technology in MFH means a re-engineering of existing services will not necessarily deliver the performance improvements required.
B. Providing re-engineered services in-house will remove the need to transfer staff to a service provider.
C. The Ministry of Food Hygiene (MFH) needs to deal with the increasing pressure to cut costs and better manage supplier's performance.
D. Relocating staff to the selected service provider's premises will mean that no property transfer is required.
E. The inadequate controls, outdated standards and outdated technology must be addressed.

Section: Business Case Theme

http://www.whatisprince2.net/prince2-theme-business-case.php

QUESTION 7
Scenario
A central government department, the Ministry of Food Hygiene (MFH), faces increasing pressure to cut costs, better manage suppliers' performance and reduce the confusion caused by inadequate internal controls, outdated standards and outdated technology. External consultants were employed to conduct a feasibility study to identify options to address the problems, and the likely costs and benefits. The following options were considered:

- Do nothing.
- Re-engineer selected business functions. Outsource selected business
- functions.

The feasibility study concluded that there was a case for outsourcing the MFH Information Technology Division and the Facilities Division (maintenance of buildings

and grounds). The recommendations were:

- One service provider should be contracted to provide the services currently provided by the Information Technology Division and the Facilities Division. A 10-year service contract should be agreed with the selected service provider.

The feasibility study developed high-level designs of the current organization, processes, systems and operating models, plus an outline Business Case for the required project. The external consultants also made the following recommendations for the management of the project:

- Use PRINCE2.
- Set up the project with 4 management stages:

Stage 1. Standard PRINCE2 initiation activities.
Stage 2. Create detailed designs (future organization, processes, systems and operating models) and the service level agreement between MFH and the future service provider.
Stage 3. Request and evaluate proposals, select service provider and agree contract.
Stage 4. Transfer equipment and staff, transfer responsibility for service provision and run trial period.

Initial estimates indicated that the project would cost £2.5m and take two years to complete.
MFH senior management agreed that there was a case for outsourcing, and accepted the recommendations as a basis for the project. There is an expected saving of £20m over 10 years.

The Outsourcing project has completed the Starting up a Project process and is now in the initiation stage. Because of the strategic importance of the project, the MFH Chief Executive Officer has taken the role of Executive. A PRINCE2-experienced Project Manager has been appointed from within MFH. Staff within the business functions being outsourced will work with the external consultants who conducted the feasibility study to define the detailed designs. Which 2 statements should be recorded under the Business options heading?

A. The re-engineering of selected business functions would not provide the required outcome.
B. The lack of up-to-date technology in MFH means a re-engineering of existing services will not necessarily deliver the performance improvements required.
C. Use external consultants to provide guidance on the detailed design of the outsourced services.
D. Set up a PRINCE2 project to deliver the outsourced services.

E. Review a list of service providers to determine a short-list of possible service providers.

Section: Business Case Theme

Reference: http://www.whatisprince2.net/prince2-theme-business-case.php

QUESTION 8
Scenario

A central government department, the Ministry of Food Hygiene (MFH), faces increasing pressure to cut costs, better manage suppliers' performance and reduce the confusion caused by inadequate internal controls, outdated standards and outdated technology. External consultants were employed to conduct a feasibility study to identify options to address the problems, and the likely costs and benefits. The following options were considered:

- Do nothing.
- Re-engineer selected business functions. Outsource selected business functions.

The feasibility study concluded that there was a case for outsourcing the MFH Information Technology Division and the Facilities Division (maintenance of buildings and grounds). The recommendations were:

- One service provider should be contracted to provide the services currently provided by the Information Technology Division and the Facilities Division. A 10-year service contract should be agreed with the selected service provider.

The feasibility study developed high-level designs of the current organization, processes, systems and operating models, plus an outline Business Case for the required project. The external consultants also made the following recommendations for the management of the project:

- Use PRINCE2.
- Set up the project with 4 management stages:

Stage 1. Standard PRINCE2 initiation activities.
Stage 2. Create detailed designs (future organization, processes, systems and operating models) and the service level agreement between MFH and the future service provider.
Stage 3. Request and evaluate proposals, select service provider and agree contract. Stage 4. Transfer equipment and staff, transfer responsibility for service provision and run trial period.

Initial estimates indicated that the project would cost £2.5m and take two years to complete.

MFH senior management agreed that there was a case for outsourcing, and accepted the recommendations as a basis for the project. There is an expected saving of £20m over 10 years.

The Outsourcing project has completed the Starting up a Project process and is now in the initiation stage. Because of the strategic importance of the project, the MFH Chief Executive Officer has taken the role of Executive. A PRINCE2-experienced Project Manager has been appointed from within MFH. Staff within the business functions being outsourced will work with the external consultants who conducted the feasibility study to define the detailed designs.

Which 2 statements should be recorded under the Expected benefits heading?

A. The 10-year outsourcing contract, at current prices, will be worth £80m.
B. Outsourcing would allow MFH to take advantage of the best services the outsourcing industry has to offer.
C. The total expected savings over 10 years, at current prices, is £20m.
D. The 10-year outsourcing contract will enable MFH to stabilize costs at agreed levels.
E. The confirmed cost of the Outsourcing project is £2.5m, but with considerable savings over 10 years.

Section: Business Case Theme

Reference: http://www.whatisprince2.net/prince2-theme-business-case.php

QUESTION 9
Scenario

A central government department, the Ministry of Food Hygiene (MFH), faces increasing pressure to cut costs, better manage suppliers' performance and reduce the confusion caused by inadequate internal controls, outdated standards and outdated technology. External consultants were employed to conduct a feasibility study to identify options to address the problems, and the likely costs and benefits. The following options were considered:

- Do nothing.
- Re-engineer selected business functions. Outsource selected business
- functions.

The feasibility study concluded that there was a case for outsourcing the MFH Information Technology Division and the Facilities Division (maintenance of buildings and grounds). The recommendations were:

One service provider should be contracted to provide the services currently provided by the Information Technology Division and the Facilities Division. A 10-year service contract should be agreed with the selected service provider.

The feasibility study developed high-level designs of the current organization, processes, systems and operating models, plus an outline Business Case for the required project. The external consultants also made the following recommendations for the management of the project:

Use PRINCE2.
Set up the project with 4 management stages:

Stage 1. Standard PRINCE2 initiation activities.
Stage 2. Create detailed designs (future organization, processes, systems and operating models) and the service level agreement between MFH and the future service provider.
Stage 3. Request and evaluate proposals, select service provider and agree contract.
Stage 4. Transfer equipment and staff, transfer responsibility for service provision and run trial period.

Initial estimates indicated that the project would cost £2.5m and take two years to complete.
MFH senior management agreed that there was a case for outsourcing, and accepted the recommendations as a basis for the project. There is an expected saving of £20m over 10 years.

The Outsourcing project has completed the Starting up a Project process and is now in the initiation stage. Because of the strategic importance of the project, the MFH Chief Executive Officer has taken the role of Executive. A PRINCE2-experienced Project Manager has been appointed from within MFH. Staff within the business functions being outsourced will work with the external consultants who conducted the feasibility study to define the detailed designs.

Which 2 statements should be recorded under the Expected dis-benefits heading?

A. An investment of £2.5m is required.
B. Staff morale will be negatively affected.
C. The project will take two years to deliver.
D. Staff may lose the opportunity to work in Information Technology.
E. MFH will lose direct control over the outsourced business functions.

Section: Business Case Theme

Reference: http://www.whatisprince2.net/prince2-theme-business-case.php

QUESTION 10
Scenario

A central government department, the Ministry of Food Hygiene (MFH), faces increasing pressure to cut costs, better manage suppliers' performance and reduce the confusion caused by inadequate internal controls, outdated standards and outdated technology. External consultants were employed to conduct a feasibility study to identify options to address the problems, and the likely costs and benefits. The following options were considered:

- Do nothing.
- Re-engineer selected business functions. Outsource selected business
- functions.

The feasibility study concluded that there was a case for outsourcing the MFH Information Technology Division and the Facilities Division (maintenance of buildings and grounds). The recommendations were:

- One service provider should be contracted to provide the services currently
- provided by the Information Technology Division and the Facilities Division. A 10-year service contract should be agreed with the selected service provider.

The feasibility study developed high-level designs of the current organization, processes, systems and operating models, plus an outline Business Case for the

required project. The external consultants also made the following recommendations for the management of the project:

- Use PRINCE2.
- Set up the project with 4 management stages:

Stage 1. Standard PRINCE2 initiation activities.
Stage 2. Create detailed designs (future organization, processes, systems and operating models) and the service level agreement between MFH and the future service provider.
Stage 3. Request and evaluate proposals, select service provider and agree contract.
Stage 4. Transfer equipment and staff, transfer responsibility for service provision and run trial period.

Initial estimates indicated that the project would cost £2.5m and take two years to complete.
MFH senior management agreed that there was a case for outsourcing, and

accepted the recommendations as a basis for the project. There is an expected saving of £20m over 10 years.

The Outsourcing project has completed the Starting up a Project process and is now in the initiation stage. Because of the strategic importance of the project, the MFH Chief Executive Officer has taken the role of Executive. A PRINCE2-experienced Project Manager has been appointed from within MFH. Staff within the business functions being outsourced will work with the external consultants who conducted the feasibility study to define the detailed designs.

Which 2 statements should be recorded under the Timescale heading?

A. The contract with the selected service provider will be agreed during stage 3.
B. The expected benefits will be calculated over 10 years from completion of the project.
C. If more MFH divisions are added to the scope of the services to be outsourced, the project timescale will be extended and the realization of benefits will be delayed.
D. The expected benefits should start to be realized as soon as the outsourced services become operational at the end of stage 4.
E. The transfer of equipment and staff is estimated to take six weeks.

Section: Business Case Theme

QUESTION 11
Scenario
A central government department, the Ministry of Food Hygiene (MFH), faces increasing pressure to cut costs, better manage suppliers' performance and reduce the confusion caused by inadequate internal controls, outdated standards and outdated technology. External consultants were employed to conduct a feasibility

study to identify options to address the problems, and the likely costs and benefits. The following options were considered:

Do nothing.
Re-engineer selected business functions. Outsource selected business functions.

The feasibility study concluded that there was a case for outsourcing the MFH Information Technology Division and the Facilities Division (maintenance of buildings and grounds). The recommendations were:

One service provider should be contracted to provide the services currently provided by the Information Technology Division and the Facilities Division. A 10-year service contract should be agreed with the selected service provider.

The feasibility study developed high-level designs of the current organization, processes, systems and operating models, plus an outline Business Case for the required project. The external consultants also made the following recommendations for the management of the project:

Use PRINCE2.
Set up the project with 4 management stages:

Stage 1. Standard PRINCE2 initiation activities.
Stage 2. Create detailed designs (future organization, processes, systems and operating models) and the service level agreement between MFH and the future service provider.
Stage 3. Request and evaluate proposals, select service provider and agree contract.
Stage 4. Transfer equipment and staff, transfer responsibility for service provision and run trial period.

Initial estimates indicated that the project would cost £2.5m and take two years to complete.
MFH senior management agreed that there was a case for outsourcing, and accepted the recommendations as a basis for the project. There is an expected saving of £20m over 10 years.

The Outsourcing project has completed the Starting up a Project process and is now in the initiation stage. Because of the strategic importance of the project, the MFH Chief Executive Officer has taken the role of Executive. A PRINCE2-experienced Project Manager has been appointed from within MFH. Staff within the business functions being outsourced will work with the external consultants who conducted the feasibility study to define the detailed designs.

Which 2 statements should be recorded under the Major risks heading?

A. Due to market conditions a suitable service provider may not be found, possibly leading to premature closure of the project.
B. Owing to employment contract changes staff may resist outsourcing, which would make it difficult to transfer staff to the selected service provider.
C. MFH's operations may be reduced and the 1a-year contract may not achieve its estimated value of £80m, which would reduce the service provider's profit.
D. The initial estimates, taken from the feasibility study report, indicate that the project will take two years to complete, which means that the business problems would remain for this period.
E. The management stages recommended by the consultants may not be appropriate, resulting in confusion in planning.

Section: Business Case Theme

QUESTION 12
HOTSPOT

Scenario

A central government department, the Ministry of Food Hygiene (MFH), faces increasing pressure to cut costs, better manage suppliers' performance and reduce the confusion caused by inadequate internal controls, outdated standards and outdated technology. External consultants were employed to conduct a feasibility study to identify options to address the problems, and the likely costs and benefits. The following options were considered:

Do nothing.
Re-engineer selected business functions. Outsource selected business functions.

The feasibility study concluded that there was a case for outsourcing the MFH Information Technology Division and the Facilities Division (maintenance of buildings and grounds). The recommendations were:

One service provider should be contracted to provide the services currently provided by the Information Technology Division and the Facilities Division. A 10-year service contract should be agreed with the selected service provider.

The feasibility study developed high-level designs of the current organization, processes, systems and operating models, plus an outline Business Case for the required project. The external consultants also made the following recommendations for the management of the project:

Use PRINCE2.
Set up the project with 4 management stages:

Stage 1. Standard PRINCE2 initiation activities.
Stage 2. Create detailed designs (future organization, processes, systems and operating models) and the service level agreement between MFH and the future service provider.

Stage 3. Request and evaluate proposals, select service provider and agree contract.
Stage 4. Transfer equipment and staff, transfer responsibility for service provision and run trial period.

Initial estimates indicated that the project would cost £2.5m and take two years to complete.
MFH senior management agreed that there was a case for outsourcing, and

accepted the recommendations as a basis for the project. There is an expected saving of £20m over 10 years.

The Outsourcing project has completed the Starting up a Project process and is now in the initiation stage. Because of the strategic importance of the project, the MFH Chief Executive Officer has taken the role of Executive. A PRINCE2-experienced Project Manager has been appointed from within MFH. Staff within the business functions being outsourced will work with the external consultants who conducted the feasibility study to define the detailed designs.

Lines 1 to 6 in the table below consist of an assertion statement and a reason statement. For each line identify the appropriate option, from options A to E, that applies. Each option can be used once, more than once or not at all.

Hot Area:

	Assertion		Reason	
1	The selected service provider should have their own Business Case for the work they are doing on the Outsourcing project.	True-False A	All project costs, including the cost of work carried out by external suppliers on the project should be included in the customer's Business Case.	True-False
2	The cost of managing the outsourcing contract should be included in the Business Case.	True-False B	The information in the Business Case is used to compare the development, maintenance and operational costs with the value of the benefits over a period of time.	True-False
3	The Business options section of the Business Case will need to be updated if the industry standards for outsourcing are changed.	True-False C	The Business options section of the Business Case describes options that have been considered to address the business problem.	True-False
4	Any expected benefit from increasing staff flexibility should be included in the Business Case.	True-False D	The Business Case should list each benefit that it is claimed would be achieved by the project's outcome.	True-False
5	The End Project Report should identify whether the expected savings of £2 over 10 years have been achieved.	True-False E	All benefits in the Business Case should be achieved before a project is closed.	True-False
6	The Project Board should ensure that the Benefits Review Plan includes the mechanisms for measuring all the claimed benefits of outsourcing.	True-False F	The Benefits Review Plan is created in the initiation stage.	True-False

Section: Business Case Theme

QUESTION 13
Which of the following is False?

A Successful project management team should.

A. Have business, user and supplier stakeholder representation
B. Never be reviewed as members should stay with the team for the duration .
C. Ensure appropriate governance by defining responsibilities for directing,

managing and delivering the project and clearly defining accountability at all levels

D. Have an effective strategy to manage communication flows to and from stakeholders

Section: Organization Theme

QUESTION 14
Which of the following statements is true of the business interest on the project?

A. Ensures the project provides value for money
B. Ensures the requirements for the project are defined
C. Ensures the products produced meet the desired quality
D. Represents the users of the product

Section: Organization Theme

QUESTION 15
Which of the following represents the four key characteristics a good Project board should display?

A. Authority, Credibility, Commitment, Availability
B. Authority, Credibility, Delegation, Availability
C. Authority, Availability, Connections, Delegation
D. Authority, Credibility, Connections, Delegation

Section: Organization Theme

QUESTION 16
Who is responsible for ensuring that Communication Management Strategy is appropriate and that planned communication activities actually take place?

A. Project Assurance
B. Project Manager
C. Corporate or Programme Management
D. Project Support

Section: Organization Theme

QUESTION 17
Which of the following roles cannot be combined?

A. Executive and Senior User
B. Project Manager and Project Support
C. Project Assurance and Team Manager
D. Senior Suppler and Supplier Assurance

Section: Organization Theme

QUESTION 18
Scenario
Additional Information

Chief Executive Officer (CEO): He started the company 25 years ago and knows his job very well. He injured his leg two years ago which has restricted his visits to the engineering area. As CEO he has an overall perspective of the business strategic requirements and the authority to commit resources as required.

Marketing Director: She has been with the company for three years, following a successful career with a publicity company. She has the ability to represent the needs of the business, particularly as this is a marketing project. She has the authority to commit the annual business marketing budget, from which the project will be funded, as she sees appropriate. She will be responsible for monitoring the expected benefits of the calendar, in particular the improvement of the company's image.

Engineering Manager: He has been responsible for many engineering innovations in the company and is still as keen and energetic as the day he started. Whilst he will not be part of the project team, his staff will feature in the photos for the promotional calendar.
Central Records: This group of five staff looks after all company records and document control. They now maintain all project files.

Bright Lights: This is the local office supplies company. It supplies all the stationery and office equipment needs of the company and will supply the stationery for this project.
Portraits ltd: This is a professional photographic company with a number of excellent photographers and a history of successful work. This company has been selected to take the photos for the company calendar. It has yet be decided which of the photographers to use.

Which 2 statements explain why the Marketing Director should be appointed as the Executive for this project?

A. She has been with the company for three years.
B. She previously had a successful career in publicity.
C. She is able to represent the business needs of MNO Manufacturing.
D. She has authority to commit the marketing budget, from which the project will be funded.
E. She requires more experience working with the engineering industry.

Section: Organization Theme

QUESTION 19
Scenario

Additional Information

Chief Executive Officer (CEO): He started the company 25 years ago and knows his job very well. He injured his leg two years ago which has restricted his visits to the engineering area. As CEO he has an overall perspective of the business strategic requirements and the authority to commit resources as required.

Marketing Director: She has been with the company for three years, following a successful career with a publicity company. She has the ability to represent the needs of the business, particularly as this is a marketing project. She has the authority to commit the annual business marketing budget, from which the project will be funded, as she sees appropriate. She will be responsible for monitoring the expected benefits of the calendar, in particular the improvement of the company's image.

Engineering Manager: He has been responsible for many engineering innovations in the company and is still as keen and energetic as the day he started. Whilst he will not be part of the project team, his staff will feature in the photos for the promotional calendar.

Central Records: This group of five staff looks after all company records and document control. They now maintain all project files.

Bright Lights: This is the local office supplies company. It supplies all the stationery and office equipment needs of the company and will supply the stationery for this project.

Portraits ltd: This is a professional photographic company with a number of excellent photographers and a history of successful work. This company has been selected to take the photos for the company calendar. It has yet been decided which of the photographers to use.

Which 2 statements explain why the CEO should be appointed as the Executive for this project?

A. He started the company 25 years ago.
B. He knows his job very well.
C. He restricts his visits to the engineering area.
D. He has the authority to commit resources as required.
E. He has an overall perspective of the business's strategic requirements.

Section: Organization Theme

QUESTION 20
Scenario
Additional Information

Chief Executive Officer (CEO): He started the company 25 years ago and knows his job very well. He injured his leg two years ago which has restricted his visits to the engineering area. As CEO he has an overall perspective of the business strategic requirements and the authority to commit resources as required.

Marketing Director: She has been with the company for three years, following a successful career with a publicity company. She has the ability to represent the needs of the business, particularly as this is a marketing project. She has the authority to commit the annual business marketing budget, from which the project will be funded, as she sees appropriate. She will be responsible for monitoring the expected benefits of the calendar, in particular the improvement of the company's image.

Engineering Manager: He has been responsible for many engineering innovations in the company and is still as keen and energetic as the day he started. Whilst he will not be part of the project team, his staff will feature in the photos for the promotional calendar.
Central Records: This group of five staff looks after all company records and document control. They now maintain all project files.

Bright Lights: This is the local office supplies company. It supplies all the stationery and office equipment needs of the company and will supply the stationery for this project.
Portraits ltd: This is a professional photographic company with a number of excellent photographers and a history of successful work. This company has been selected to take the photos for the company calendar. It has yet been decided which of the photographers to use.

Which 2 statements explain why the Marketing Director should be appointed as a Senior User for this project?

A. She can represent the Marketing department.
B. She previously had a successful career in publicity.
C. The Marketing department will help to deliver the benefits of this project.
D. The project will be funded from the business marketing budget.
E. A number of the products will be produced by the Sales department and the Marketing department.

Section: Organization Theme

QUESTION 21
Scenario
Additional Information

Chief Executive Officer (CEO): He started the company 25 years ago and knows his job very well. He injured his leg two years ago which has restricted his visits to the engineering area. As CEO he has an overall perspective of the business strategic requirements and the authority to commit resources as required.

Marketing Director: She has been with the company for three years, following a successful career with a publicity company. She has the ability to represent the needs of the business, particularly as this is a marketing project. She has the authority to commit the annual business marketing budget, from which the project will be funded, as she sees appropriate. She will be responsible for monitoring the expected benefits of the calendar, in particular the improvement of the company's

image.

Engineering Manager: He has been responsible for many engineering innovations in the company and is still as keen and energetic as the day he started. Whilst he will not be part of the project team, his staff will feature in the photos for the promotional calendar.
Central Records: This group of five staff looks after all company records and document control. They now maintain all project files.

Bright Lights: This is the local office supplies company. It supplies all the stationery and office equipment needs of the company and will supply the stationery for this project.
Portraits ltd: This is a professional photographic company with a number of excellent photographers and a history of successful work. This company has been

selected to take the photos for the company calendar. It has yet be decided which of the photographers to use.

Which 2 statements explain why the Sales Manager should be appointed as a Senior User for this project?

A. He joined the company last year with huge enthusiasm.
B. He would like to move into the Marketing department in the future and sees this as an opportunity to work closely with the Marketing Director.
C. The launch of a company calendar will impact the Sales department.
D. He reports directly to the Marketing Director.
E. He is able to represent current and prospective customer interests.

Section: Organization Theme

QUESTION 22
Scenario
Additional Information

Chief Executive Officer (CEO): He started the company 25 years ago and knows his job very well. He injured his leg two years ago which has restricted his visits to the engineering area. As CEO he has an overall perspective of the business strategic requirements and the authority to commit resources as required.

Marketing Director: She has been with the company for three years, following a successful career with a publicity company. She has the ability to represent the needs of the business, particularly as this is a marketing project. She has the authority to commit the annual business marketing budget, from which the project will be funded, as she sees appropriate. She will be responsible for monitoring the expected benefits of the calendar, in particular the improvement of the company's image.

Engineering Manager: He has been responsible for many engineering innovations in the company and is still as keen and energetic as the day he started. Whilst he will not be part of the project team, his staff will feature in the photos for the promotional calendar.

Central Records: This group of five staff looks after all company records and document control. They now maintain all project files.

Bright Lights: This is the local office supplies company. It supplies all the stationery and office equipment needs of the company and will supply the stationery for this project.
Portraits ltd: This is a professional photographic company with a number of

excellent photographers and a history of successful work. This company has been selected to take the photos for the company calendar. It has yet to be decided which of the photographers to use.

Which 2 statements explain why the Purchasing Manager should be appointed as a Senior Supplier for this project?

A. He is responsible for the organization's procurement activates.
B. He is responsible for the performance of supplier contracts.
C. He was an engineer and worked in that area before taking up his current position.
D. He can influence the external supplier's Business Case.
E. He is not appropriate for the role of Executive or Senior User.

Section: Organization Theme

QUESTION 23
Scenario
Additional Information

Chief Executive Officer (CEO): He started the company 25 years ago and knows his job very well. He injured his leg two years ago which has restricted his visits to the engineering area. As CEO he has an overall perspective of the business strategic requirements and the authority to commit resources as required.

Marketing Director: She has been with the company for three years, following a successful career with a publicity company. She has the ability to represent the needs of the business, particularly as this is a marketing project. She has the authority to commit the annual business marketing budget, from which the project will be funded, as she sees appropriate. She will be responsible for monitoring the expected benefits of the calendar, in particular the improvement of the company's image.

Engineering Manager: He has been responsible for many engineering innovations in the company and is still as keen and energetic as the day he started. VVhilst he will not be part of the project team, his staff will feature in the photos for the promotional calendar.
Central Records: This group of five staff looks after all company records and document control. They now maintain all project files.

Bright Lights: This is the local office supplies company. It supplies all the stationery and office equipment needs of the company and will supply the stationery for this project.
Portraits ltd: This is a professional photographic company with a number of excellent photographers and a history of successful work. This company has been

selected to take the photos for the company calendar. It has yet to be decided which of the photographers to use.

Which 2 statements explain why the Sales Manager should be appointed as User Assurance for this project?

A. He joined the company last year with huge enthusiasm and is keen to increase sales.
B. He can provide an evaluation of the potential impact the calendar will have on sales.
C. He is able to advise on suitable stakeholder engagement of current and prospective customers.
D. He would like to move into the Marketing department in the future and sees this as an opportunity to work closely with the Marketing Director.
E. He can resolve any conflict in requirements between the Sales department and the Marketing department.

Section: Organization Theme

QUESTION 24
Scenario
Additional Information

Chief Executive Officer (CEO): He started the company 25 years ago and knows his job very well. He injured his leg two years ago which has restricted his visits to the engineering area. As CEO he has an overall perspective of the business strategic requirements and the authority to commit resources as required.

Marketing Director: She has been with the company for three years, following a successful career with a publicity company. She has the ability to represent the needs of the business, particularly as this is a marketing project. She has the authority to commit the annual business marketing budget, from which the project will be funded, as she sees appropriate. She will be responsible for monitoring the expected benefits of the calendar, in particular the improvement of the company's image.

Engineering Manager: He has been responsible for many engineering innovations in the company and is still as keen and energetic as the day he started. Whilst he will not be part of the project team, his staff will feature in the photos for the promotional calendar.

Central Records: This group of five staff looks after all company records and document control. They now maintain all project files.

Bright Lights: This is the local office supplies company. It supplies all the stationery and office equipment needs of the company and will supply the stationery for this project.

Portraits ltd: This is a professional photographic company with a number of excellent photographers and a history of successful work. This company has been selected to take the photos for the company calendar. It has yet to be decided which of the photographers to use.

Which 2 statements explain why Central Records should be appointed as Project Support for this project?

A. They control the receipt, identification, versions, storage and issue of all project products within the company's projects.
B. They already exist within the organization and have been with the company for many years.
C. They will ensure compliance with all company policies and procedures.
D. They perform a quality assurance function across all projects.
E. They have knowledge of the organizational standards that will be applicable to the project.

Section: Organization Theme

QUESTION 25
Scenario
Additional Information

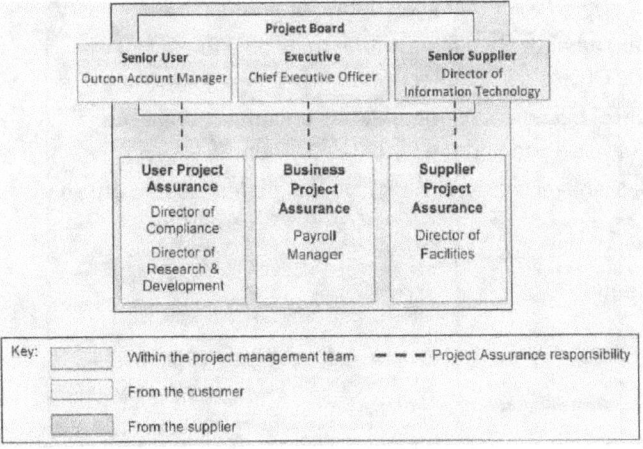

Further information on some resources who could be involved in the project:

Outcome Account Manager: He represents Outcome which is a recruitment agency that provides specialist outsourcing resources. Outcome provided the consultants who carried out the feasibility study and the same consultants will be providing support and guidance to the Information Technology and Facilities teams during the project.

Director of Finance Division: She was transferred from the Information Technology Division 12 months ago. She is responsible for ensuring a cost-conscious approach is adopted in all operational and project activities across the Ministry of Food Hygiene.

Hardware Manager: Reports to the Director of Information Technology. He provides computer hardware to all business functions but has little awareness of the needs of his colleagues working in software.

Payroll Manager: Reports to the Director of Finance. He is a very experienced and efficient qualified accountant who has much of the responsibility of running the Finance Division on behalf of the Director of Finance. He has been involved in drafting the Ministry's business strategy and assisting in a full business risk assessment. He also drafted the corporate Business Case standards.

Which 2 alternative actions apply to the proposed Executive for this project?

A. Retain because he accepts that outsourcing is the best solution.
B. Replace with 'Director of Finance Division' because she can ensure a cost-conscious approach to the project that gives value for money.
C. Retain because he has the right level of authority to be able to control the strategic nature of the Outsourcing project.
D. Add 'Director of Finance' because she understands the operation of the Information Technology Division and the Facilities Division.
E. Replace with 'Payroll Manager' because he is a very experienced and efficient qualified accountant.

Section: Organization Theme

QUESTION 26
Scenario
Additional Information

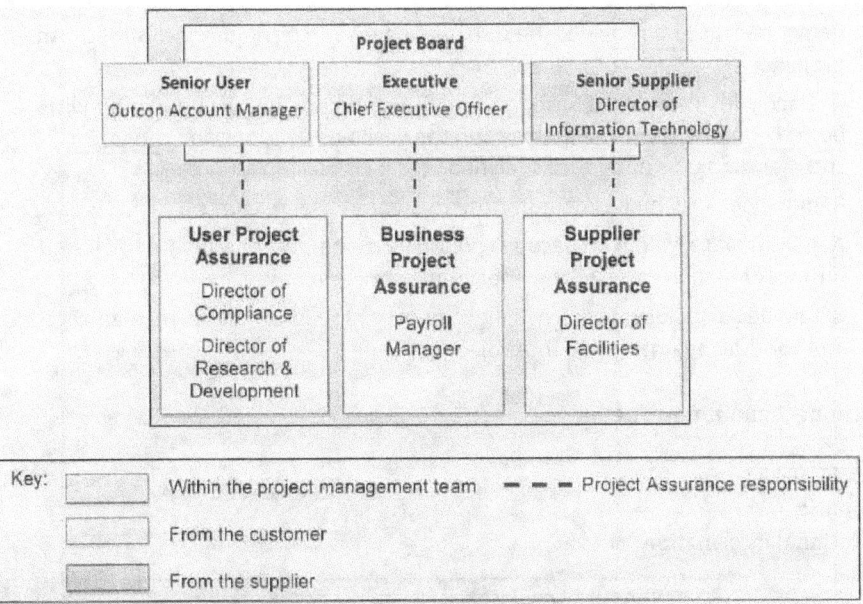

Further information on some resources who could be involved in the project:

Outcome Account Manager: He represents Outcome which is a recruitment agency that provides specialist outsourcing resources. Outcome provided the consultants who carried out the feasibility study and the same consultants will be providing support and guidance to the Information Technology and Facilities teams during the project.

Director of Finance Division: She was transferred from the Information Technology Division 12 months ago. She is responsible for ensuring a cost-conscious approach is adopted in all operational and project activities across the Ministry of Food Hygiene.

Hardware Manager: Reports to the Director of Information Technology. He provides computer hardware to all business functions but has little awareness of the needs of his colleagues working in software.

Payroll Manager: Reports to the Director of Finance. He is a very experienced and efficient qualified accountant who has much of the responsibility of running the Finance Division on behalf of the Director of Finance. He has been involved in drafting the Ministry's business strategy and assisting in a full business risk assessment. He also drafted the corporate Business Case standards.

Which 2 alternative actions apply to the proposed Senior User for this project?

A. Retain because he provides the outsourcing resources required to support the project.
B. Replace with 'Director of Research and Development' because she deals with both the Information Technology and the Facilities Divisions and can make sure her division's needs are specified.
C. Remove because he has no authority to commit user resources.
D. Add 'Hardware Manager' because he provides computer hardware to all business functions and will be impacted by the outcome.
E. Retain because he will be providing support to the Information Technology and Facilities teams during the project.

Section: Organization Theme

QUESTION 27
Scenario
Additional Information

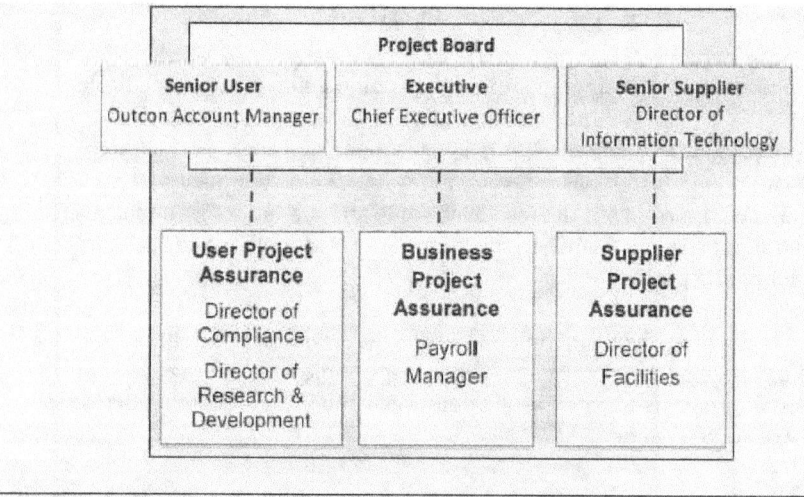

Further information on some resources who could be involved in the project:

Outcome Account Manager: He represents Outcome which is a recruitment agency that provides specialist outsourcing resources. Outcome provided the consultants who carried out the feasibility study and the same consultants will be providing support and guidance to the Information Technology and Facilities teams during the project.

Director of Finance Division: She was transferred from the Information Technology Division 12 months ago. She is responsible for ensuring a cost-conscious approach is adopted in all operational and project activities across the Ministry of Food Hygiene.

Hardware Manager: Reports to the Director of Information Technology. He provides computer hardware to all business functions but has little awareness of the needs of his colleagues working in software.

Payroll Manager: Reports to the Director of Finance. He is a very experienced and efficient qualified accountant who has much of the responsibility of running the Finance Division on behalf of the Director of Finance. He has been involved in drafting the Ministry's business strategy and assisting in a full business risk assessment. He also drafted the corporate Business Case standards.

Which 2 alternative actions apply to the proposed Senior Supplier for this project?

A. Retain because she is responsible for the design of the future Information Technology organization and working practices.
B. Add 'Director of Facilities' because he is responsible for the design of the future organization, processes, systems and operation models for Facilities.
C. Add 'Hardware Manager' because he provides computer hardware to all business functions and will be impacted by the outcome.
D. Remove because she only represents the Information Technology Division.
E. Replace with 'Director of Facilities' because he supports the initiative and has many ideas about how to improve the service.

Section: Organization Theme

QUESTION 28
Scenario
Additional Information

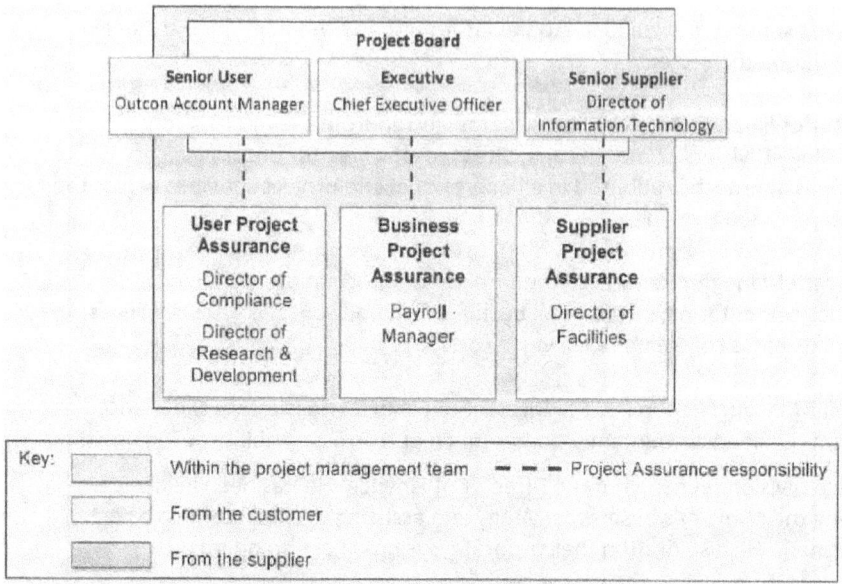

Further information on some resources who could be involved in the project:

Outcome Account Manager: He represents Outcome which is a recruitment agency that provides specialist outsourcing resources. Outcome provided the consultants who carried out the feasibility study and the same consultants will be providing support and guidance to the Information Technology and Facilities teams during the project.

Director of Finance Division: She was transferred from the Information Technology Division 12 months ago. She is responsible for ensuring a cost-conscious approach is adopted in all operational and project activities across the Ministry of Food Hygiene.

Hardware Manager: Reports to the Director of Information Technology. He provides computer hardware to all business functions but has little awareness of the needs of his colleagues working in software.

Payroll Manager: Reports to the Director of Finance. He is a very experienced and efficient qualified accountant who has much of the responsibility of running the

Finance Division on behalf of the Director of Finance. He has been involved in drafting the Ministry's business strategy and assisting in a full business risk assessment. He also drafted the corporate Business Case standards.

Which 2 alternative actions apply to the proposed business assurance for this project?

A. Remove because he will be impacted by the project and therefore represents a user.
B. Replace with 'Project Manager' because this is a simple project that does not require additional business assurance.
C. Add Outcome Consultants' because they carried out the feasibility study.
D. Add 'Director of Finance Division' because she is responsible for checking that any supplier and contractor payments are authorized.
E. Retain because he is familiar with the Ministry of Food Hygiene business strategy, the business level risk assessment and the Business Case standards.

Section: Organization Theme

QUESTION 29
Scenario
Additional Information

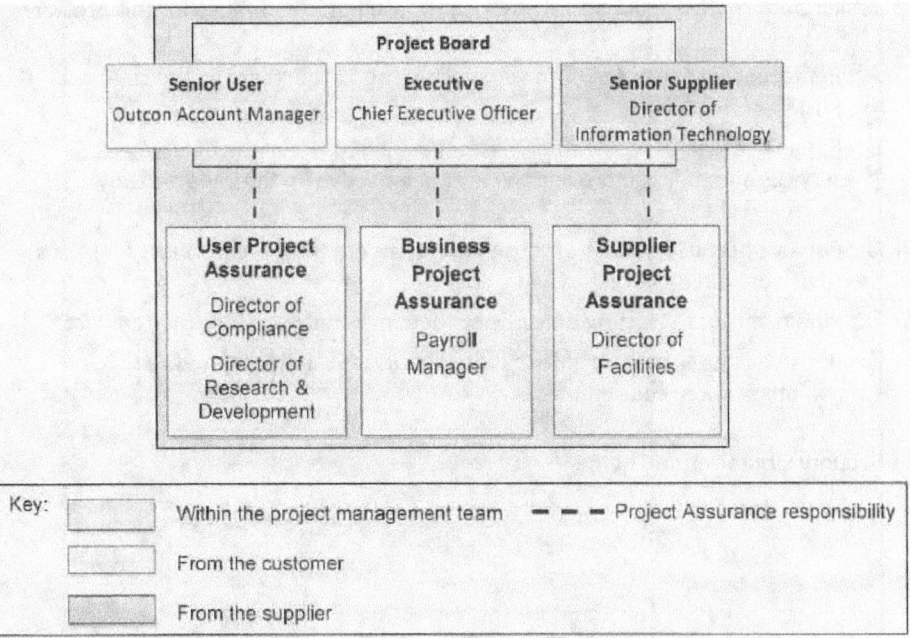

Further information on some resources who could be involved in the project:

Outcome Account Manager: He represents Outcome which is a recruitment agency that provides specialist outsourcing resources. Outcome provided the consultants who carried out the feasibility study and the same consultants will be providing support and guidance to the Information Technology and Facilities teams during the project.

Director of Finance Division: She was transferred from the Information Technology Division 12 months ago. She is responsible for ensuring a cost-conscious approach is adopted in all operational and project activities across the Ministry of Food Hygiene.

Hardware Manager: Reports to the Director of Information Technology. He provides computer hardware to all business functions but has little awareness of the needs of his colleagues working in software.

Payroll Manager: Reports to the Director of Finance. He is a very experienced and efficient qualified accountant who has much of the responsibility of running the Finance Division on behalf of the Director of Finance. He has been involved in drafting the Ministry's business strategy and assisting in a full business risk assessment. He also drafted the corporate Business Case standards.

Which 2 alternative actions apply to the proposed user assurance for this project?

A. Retain because they are both very positive about outsourcing the selected business functions.
B. Retain because their divisions will be the major users of the outsourced services and they can provide the user perspective on the impact of any proposed changes.
C. Remove because neither of these individuals are from the business functions to be outsourced.
D. Retain because selecting only one of them may cause unnecessary conflict.
E. Retain because they are able to help identify stakeholders and their communication requirements.

Section: Organization Theme

QUESTION 30
Project Scenario – Health and Safety Training Project:

ABC Company is a well-established training company that uses a standard model to develop training materials and deliver courses to customers.

ABC Company has commissioned a project in response to recent changes in government legislation relating to health and safety on construction sites. The project will deliver "capability to provide health and safety training", including the materials needed for classroom-based training and e-learning. The expected benefits for construction companies include a reduction in lost days and legal costs due to accidents.

The e-learning course will be developed by a specialist external consultancy. The materials for classroom-based training will be delivered by ABC Company's development team. All course materials will be piloted before they are used. ABC Company will deliver training to its customers and also hopes to sell the course materials to other training companies as part of their operational business. ABC Company will use their own sales and marketing departments to promote the courses.

The legislation requires construction companies to comply with the new legislation within two years. The course materials and trainers have to be accredited by a government agency before courses can be delivered. ABC Company is planning to deliver pilot courses within five months of starting the project.

The ABC Company standard development model for new courses recommends the following stages:

Stage 1	Initiation stage
Stage 2	Classroom-based training materials Marketing materials Training venue specifications Accredited classroom-based course
Stage 3	E-learning course Amended course booking procedures Marketed courses Planned pilot courses Updated corporate quality procedures Accredited e-learning course Accredited trainers
Stage 4	Delivered pilot courses Finalized materials Project product: Capability to provide health and safety training

End of the Project scenario.

Additional Information:

The Chief Executive Officer (CEO) founded the company five years ago. Under her leadership, ABC Company has grown quickly into a successful training company. It delivers a range of accredited professional training.

The Finance Director is also a founder member of ABC Company and is responsible for authorizing budgets for the Operations and Development Teams. She authorizes all large contracts personally.

The Purchasing Manager reports to the Finance Director and is responsible for managing and monitoring supplier contracts.

The Operations Director is responsible for the delivery off all training and for the training development budget. His department organizes courses, venues and trainers. They work with the Product and the Sales teams to provide a comprehensive training schedule. ABC Company's IT manager reports to the Operations Director.

The Business Development Director has recently been appointed to identify new training needs and propose new products. She will work with the Operations. Director to ensure a cost-conscious approach and that appropriate development technologies are used for the health and safety course.

The Training Development Manager reports to the Business Development Director and is responsible for developing training materials and gaining accreditation, in

accordance with the standard course development model. Course developers in his team have skills in a range of development technologies and are allocated to projects as needed.

The Training Delivery Manager, who reports to the Operations Director, is responsible for ensuring that internal and external trainers deliver ABC Company training courses to the required standard. He also checks course materials to ensure they are fit for purpose and of the required quality.

The Central Services Director has responsibility for corporate communications, facilities management and configuration management. He recently led a project to consolidate all company quality systems into one quality management system and set up a corporate quality department, now managed by the Corporate Quality Manager.

The Corporate Document Manager reports to the Central Services Director. She

helped establish the company's document management system and now operates it across the business. She manages a team of administrators and contracts staff when workload is high.

The Sales Director joined ABC Company two months ago and is keen to establish himself by suggesting new markets for the courses and material. All account managers and the marketing team report to him. They promote existing training courses to other training companies and existing customers.

End of the additional information.

A construction company that is one of ABC Company's key clients has agreed to provide a member of the staff to review and comment on the 'e-learning course'. Which stakeholder interest should the member of staff represent, and why?

A. Supplier, because this stakeholder provides the expertise required by the project.
B. Supplier, because this stakeholder is an external supplier.
C. User, because this stakeholder may train its staff using the 'e-learning course'.
D. User, because this stakeholder ensures that the project provides value for money.

Section: Organization Theme

QUESTION 31
Project Scenario – Health and Safety Training Project:

ABC Company is a well-established training company that uses a standard model to develop training materials and deliver courses to customers.

ABC Company has commissioned a project in response to recent changes in government legislation relating to health and safety on construction sites. The project will deliver "capability to provide health and safety training", including the materials needed for classroom-based training and e-learning. The expected benefits for construction companies include a reduction in lost days and legal costs due to accidents.

The e-learning course will be developed by a specialist external consultancy. The materials for classroom-based training will be delivered by ABC Company's development team. All course materials will be piloted before they are used. ABC Company will deliver training to its customers and also hopes to sell the course materials to other training companies as part of their operational business. ABC . Company will use their own sales and marketing departments to promote the courses.

The legislation requires construction companies to comply with the new legislation within two years. The course materials and trainers have to be accredited by a government agency before courses can be delivered. ABC Company is planning to deliver pilot courses within five months of starting the project.

The ABC Company standard development model for new courses recommends the following stages:

Stage 1	Initiation stage
Stage 2	Classroom-based training materials Marketing materials Training venue specifications Accredited classroom-based course
Stage 3	E-learning course Amended course booking procedures Marketed courses Planned pilot courses Updated corporate quality procedures Accredited e-learning course Accredited trainers
Stage 4	Delivered pilot courses Finalized materials Project product: Capability to provide health and safety training

End of the Project scenario.

Additional Information:

The <u>Chief Executive Officer (CEO)</u> founded the company five years ago. Under her leadership, ABC Company has grown quickly into a successful training company. It delivers a range of accredited professional training.

The <u>Finance Director</u> is also a founder member of ABC Company and is responsible for authorizing budgets for the Operations and Development Teams. She authorizes all large contracts personally.

The <u>Purchasing Manager</u> reports to the Finance Director and is responsible for managing and monitoring supplier contracts.

The <u>Operations Director</u> is responsible for the delivery off all training and for the training development budget. His department organizes courses, venues and trainers. They work with the Product and the Sales teams to provide a comprehensive training schedule. ABC Company's IT manager reports to the Operations Director.

The Business Development Director has recently been appointed to identify new training needs and propose new products. She will work with the Operations Director to ensure a cost-conscious approach and that appropriate development technologies are used for the health and safety course.

The Training Development Manager reports to the Business Development Director and is responsible for developing training materials and gaining accreditation, in accordance with the standard course development model. Course developers in his team have skills in a range of development technologies and are allocated to projects as needed.

The Training Delivery Manager, who reports to the Operations Director, is responsible for ensuring that internal and external trainers deliver ABC Company training courses to the required standard. He also checks course materials to ensure they are fit for purpose and of the required quality.

The Central Services Director has responsibility for corporate communications, facilities management and configuration management. He recently led a project to consolidate all company quality systems into one quality management system and set up a corporate quality department, now managed by the Corporate Quality Manager.

The Corporate Document Manager reports to the Central Services Director. She helped establish the company's document management system and now operates it across the business. She manages a team of administrators and contracts staff when workload is high.

The Sales Director joined ABC Company two months ago and is keen to establish himself by suggesting new markets for the courses and material. All account managers and the marketing team report to him. They promote existing training courses to other training companies and existing customers.

End of the additional information.

Use the 'Additional Information' in the Scenario Booklet to answer this question. The Operations Director is the executive for the project and has proposed that a senior course developer be appointed as project manager. The course developer works in the Training Development Manager's team and has a good understanding of the standard course development model. The course developer was a team manager on a previous project for which the Operations Director was the executive.
Is this proposed appointment appropriate, and why?

A. Yes, because the course developer is responsible for ensuring that trainers deliver courses to the required standard.
B. Yes, because the course developer is likely to have the project management and specialist knowledge required.
C. No, because the course developer's team reports to the Business Development Director, not the Operations Director.
D. No, because there is a conflict of interest as the Training Development Manager is responsible for gaining accreditation.

Section: Organization Theme

QUESTION 32
Project Scenario – Health and Safety Training Project:

ABC Company is a well-established training company that uses a standard model to develop training materials and deliver courses to customers.

ABC Company has commissioned a project in response to recent changes in government legislation relating to health and safety on construction sites. The project will deliver "capability to provide health and safety training", including the materials needed for classroom-based training and e-learning. The expected benefits for construction companies include a reduction in lost days and legal costs due to accidents.

The e-learning course will be developed by a specialist external consultancy. The materials for classroom-based training will be delivered by ABC Company's development team. All course materials will be piloted before they are used. ABC Company will deliver training to its customers and also hopes to sell the course materials to other training companies as part of their operational business. ABC Company will use their own sales and marketing departments to promote the courses.

The legislation requires construction companies to comply with the new legislation within two years. The course materials and trainers have to be accredited by a government agency before courses can be delivered. ABC Company is planning to deliver pilot courses within five months of starting the project.

The ABC Company standard development model for new courses recommends the following stages:

End of the Project scenario.
Additional Information:

The Chief Executive Officer (CEO) founded the company five years ago. Under her leadership, ABC Company has grown quickly into a successful training company. It delivers a range of accredited professional training.

The Finance Director is also a founder member of ABC Company and is responsible for authorizing budgets for the Operations and Development Teams. She authorizes all large contracts personally.

The Purchasing Manager reports to the Finance Director and is responsible for managing and monitoring supplier contracts.

The Operations Director is responsible for the delivery off all training and for the training development budget. His department organizes courses, venues and trainers. They work with the Product and the Sales teams to provide a comprehensive training schedule. ABC Company's IT manager reports to the Operations Director.

The Business Development Director has recently been appointed to identify new training needs and propose new products. She will work with the Operations. Director to ensure a cost-conscious approach and that appropriate development technologies are used for the health and safety course.

The Training Development Manager reports to the Business Development Director and is responsible for developing training materials and gaining accreditation, in accordance with the standard course development model. Course developers in his team have skills in a range of development technologies and are allocated to projects as needed.

The Training Delivery Manager, who reports to the Operations Director, is responsible for ensuring that internal and external trainers deliver ABC Company training courses to the required standard. He also checks course materials to ensure they are fit for purpose and of the required quality.

The Central Services Director has responsibility for corporate communications, facilities management and configuration management. He recently led a project to consolidate all company quality systems into one quality management system and set up a corporate quality department, now managed by the Corporate Quality Manager.

The Corporate Document Manager reports to the Central Services Director. She helped establish the company's document management system and now operates it across the business. She manages a team of administrators and contracts staff when workload is high.

The Sales Director joined ABC Company two months ago and is keen to establish himself by suggesting new markets for the courses and material. All account managers and the marketing team report to him. They promote existing training

courses to other training companies and existing customers.
End of the additional information.

The 'classroom-based training materials' will be used as the basis for developing the 'e-learning course'. As a result, the executive wants to ensure that the 'classroom-based training materials' are of the required standard. The executive has asked to meet the project manager every day during stage 2 to discuss progress and identify any concerns regarding quality.

Is this an appropriate approach to applying the organization theme, and why?

A. Yes, because the executive should be available to provide ad hoc direction to the project manager.
B. Yes, because the executive should be the key decision-maker on the project, supported by other project board members.
C. No, because the senior user should be responsible for specifying the quality criteria for the training materials.
D. No, because the project manager should be given authority to manage the project on a day-to-day basis.

Section: Organization Theme

QUESTION 33

Project Scenario – Health and Safety Training Project:

ABC Company is a well-established training company that uses a standard model to develop training materials and deliver courses to customers.

ABC Company has commissioned a project in response to recent changes in government legislation relating to health and safety on construction sites. The project will deliver "capability to provide health and safety training", including the materials needed for classroom-based training and e-learning. The expected benefits for construction companies include a reduction in lost days and legal costs due to accidents.

The e-learning course will be developed by a specialist external consultancy. The materials for classroom-based training will be delivered by ABC Company's development team. All course materials will be piloted before they are used. ABC Company will deliver training to its customers and also hopes to sell the course materials to other training companies as part of their operational business. ABC Company will use their own sales and marketing departments to promote the courses.

The legislation requires construction companies to comply with the new legislation within two years. The course materials and trainers have to be accredited by a government agency before courses can be delivered. ABC Company is planning to deliver pilot courses within five months of starting the project.

The ABC Company standard development model for new courses recommends the following stages:

End of the Project scenario.

Additional Information:

The Chief Executive Officer (CEO) founded the company five years ago. Under her leadership, ABC Company has grown quickly into a successful training company. It delivers a range of accredited professional training.

The Finance Director is also a founder member of ABC Company and is responsible for authorizing budgets for the Operations and Development Teams. She authorizes all large contracts personally.

The Purchasing Manager reports to the Finance Director and is responsible for managing and monitoring supplier contracts.

The Operations Director is responsible for the delivery off all training and for the training development budget. His department organizes courses, venues and trainers. They work with the Product and the Sales teams to provide a comprehensive training schedule. ABC Company's IT manager reports to the Operations Director.

The Business Development Director has recently been appointed to identify new training needs and propose new products. She will work with the Operations. Director to ensure a cost-conscious approach and that appropriate development technologies are used for the health and safety course.

The Training Development Manager reports to the Business Development Director and is responsible for developing training materials and gaining accreditation, in accordance with the standard course development model. Course developers in his team have skills in a range of development technologies and are allocated to projects as needed.

The Training Delivery Manager, who reports to the Operations Director, is responsible for ensuring that internal and external trainers deliver ABC Company training

courses to the required standard. He also checks course materials to ensure they are fit for purpose and of the required quality.

The Central Services Director has responsibility for corporate communications, facilities management and configuration management. He recently led a project to consolidate all company quality systems into one quality management system and set up a corporate quality department, now managed by the Corporate Quality Manager.

The Corporate Document Manager reports to the Central Services Director. She helped establish the company's document management system and now operates it across the business. She manages a team of administrators and contracts staff when workload is high.

The Sales Director joined ABC Company two months ago and is keen to establish himself by suggesting new markets for the courses and material. All account managers and the marketing team report to him. They promote existing training courses to other training companies and existing customers.

End of the additional information.

ABC Company has a number of projects in progress. The executive of the Health and Safety Training Project is also a member of the project board for two other projects and is very busy. As a result, during this initiation stage, the executive has appointed another person to carry out both their business assurance and the role of change authority for minor and medium severity issues.
Is this appropriate, and why?

A. Yes, because people with delegated project assurance roles may act as the change authority.
B. Yes, because projects that are likely to have many changes should delegate the change authority.
C. No, because the decision to have a change authority should be made before the project is authorized.
D. No, because the project manager identifies the level of tailoring that is relevant for the project.

Section: Organization Theme

QUESTION 34
DRAG DROP

Project Scenario – Health and Safety Training Project:

ABC Company is a well-established training company that uses a standard model to develop training materials and deliver courses to customers.

ABC Company has commissioned a project in response to recent changes in government legislation relating to health and safety on construction sites. The project will deliver "capability to provide health and safety training", including the materials needed for classroom-based training and e-learning. The expected benefits for construction companies include a reduction in lost days and legal costs due to accidents.

The e-learning course will be developed by a specialist external consultancy. The materials for classroom-based training will be delivered by ABC Company's development team. All course materials will be piloted before they are used. ABC Company will deliver training to its customers and also hopes to sell the course materials to other training companies as part of their operational business. ABC Company will use their own sales and marketing departments to promote the courses.

The legislation requires construction companies to comply with the new legislation within two years. The course materials and trainers have to be accredited by a government agency before courses can be delivered. ABC Company is planning to deliver pilot courses within five months of starting the project.

The ABC Company standard development model for new courses recommends the following stages:

Stage 1	Initiation stage
Stage 2	Classroom-based training materials Marketing materials Training venue specifications Accredited classroom-based course
Stage 3	E-learning course Amended course booking procedures Marketed courses Planned pilot courses Updated corporate quality procedures Accredited e-learning course Accredited trainers
Stage 4	Delivered pilot courses Finalized materials Project product: Capability to provide health and safety training

End of the Project scenario.

Additional Information:

The Chief Executive Officer (CEO) founded the company five years ago. Under her leadership, ABC Company has grown quickly into a successful training company. It delivers a range of accredited professional training.

The Finance Director is also a founder member of ABC Company and is responsible for authorizing budgets for the Operations and Development Teams. She authorizes all large contracts personally.

The Purchasing Manager reports to the Finance Director and is responsible for managing and monitoring supplier contracts.

The Operations Director is responsible for the delivery off all training and for the training development budget. His department organizes courses, venues and trainers. They work with the Product and the Sales teams to provide a comprehensive training schedule. ABC Company's IT manager reports to the Operations Director.

The Business Development Director has recently been appointed to identify new training needs and propose new products. She will work with the Operations. Director to ensure a cost-conscious approach and that appropriate development technologies are used for the health and safety course.

The Training Development Manager reports to the Business Development Director and is responsible for developing training materials and gaining accreditation, in accordance with the standard course development model. Course developers in his team have skills in a range of development technologies and are allocated to projects as needed.

The Training Delivery Manager, who reports to the Operations Director, is responsible for ensuring that internal and external trainers deliver ABC Company training courses to the required standard. He also checks course materials to ensure they are fit for purpose and of the required quality.

The Central Services Director has responsibility for corporate communications, facilities management and configuration management. He recently led a project to consolidate all company quality systems into one quality management system and set up a corporate quality department, now managed by the Corporate Quality Manager.

The <u>Corporate Document Manager</u> reports to the Central Services Director. She helped establish the company's document management system and now operates it across the business. She manages a team of administrators and contracts staff when workload is high.

The <u>Sales Director</u> joined ABC Company two months ago and is keen to establish himself by suggesting new markets for the courses and material. All account managers and the marketing team report to him. They promote existing training courses to other training companies and existing customers.
End of the additional information. ORGANIZATION

The communication management approach is being developed. ABC Company's corporate management has agreed the information about proposed courses can be shared externally, provided that a non-disclosure agreement is signed and corporate management is informed.
Here are three items of information relating to the sharing of course materials. Under which heading of the communication management approach (A-F) should they be included?
Choose only one heading for each item of information. Each heading can be used once, more than once, or not at all.

Select and Place:

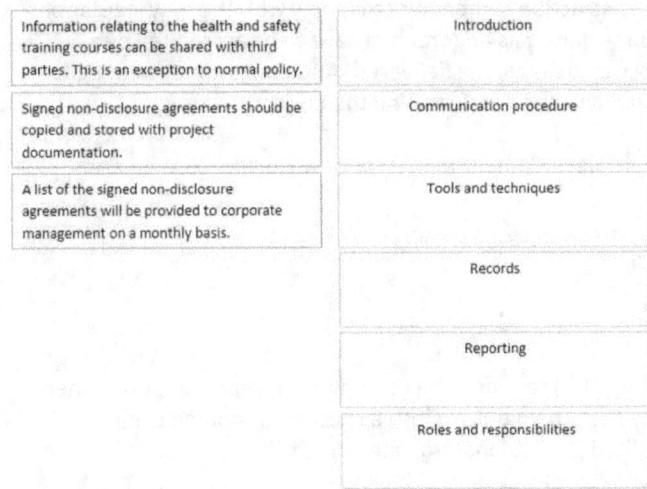

Section: Organization Theme

QUESTION 35
Project Scenario – Health and Safety Training Project:

ABC Company is a well-established training company that uses a standard model to develop training materials and deliver courses to customers.

ABC Company has commissioned a project in response to recent changes in government legislation relating to health and safety on construction sites. The project will deliver "capability to provide health and safety training", including the materials needed for classroom-based training and e-learning. The expected benefits for construction companies include a reduction in lost days and legal costs due to accidents.

The e-learning course will be developed by a specialist external consultancy. The materials for classroom-based training will be delivered by ABC Company's development team. All course materials will be piloted before they are used. ABC Company will deliver training to its customers and also hopes to sell the course materials to other training companies as part of their operational business. ABC Company will use their own sales and marketing departments to promote the courses.

The legislation requires construction companies to comply with the new legislation within two years. The course materials and trainers have to be accredited by a government agency before courses can be delivered. ABC Company is planning to deliver pilot courses within five months of starting the project.

The ABC Company standard development model for new courses recommends the following stages:

End of the Project scenario.

Additional Information:

The <u>Chief Executive Officer (CEO)</u> founded the company five years ago. Under her leadership, ABC Company has grown quickly into a successful training company. It delivers a range of accredited professional training.

The <u>Finance Director</u> is also a founder member of ABC Company and is responsible for authorizing budgets for the Operations and Development Teams. She authorizes all large contracts personally.

The <u>Purchasing Manager</u> reports to the Finance Director and is responsible for managing and monitoring supplier contracts.

The <u>Operations Director</u> is responsible for the delivery off all training and for the

training development budget. His department organizes courses, venues and trainers. They work with the Product and the Sales teams to provide a comprehensive training schedule. ABC Company's IT manager reports to the Operations Director.

The <u>Business Development Director</u> has recently been appointed to identify new training needs and propose new products. She will work with the Operations. Director to ensure a cost-conscious approach and that appropriate development technologies are used for the health and safety course.

The <u>Training Development Manager</u> reports to the Business Development Director and is responsible for developing training materials and gaining accreditation, in accordance with the standard course development model. Course developers in his team have skills in a range of development technologies and are allocated to projects as needed.

The <u>Training Delivery Manager</u>, who reports to the Operations Director, is responsible for ensuring that internal and external trainers deliver ABC Company training courses to the required standard. He also checks course materials to ensure they are fit for purpose and of the required quality.

The <u>Central Services Director</u> has responsibility for corporate communications, facilities management and configuration management. He recently led a project to consolidate all company quality systems into one quality management system and set up a corporate quality department, now managed by the Corporate Quality Manager.

The <u>Corporate Document Manager</u> reports to the Central Services Director. She helped establish the company's document management system and now operates it across the business. She manages a team of administrators and contracts staff when workload is high.

The <u>Sales Director</u> joined ABC Company two months ago and is keen to establish himself by suggesting new markets for the courses and material. All account managers and the marketing team report to him. They promote existing training courses to other training companies and existing customers.

End of the additional information.

The development of the 'e-learning course' will be outsourced to an external supplier and their key members will join the project management team. The supplier wants to keep their work processes confidential and not share these with ABC Company. ABC Company has agreed.

Who should approve the external supplier's team plan?

A. Senior supplier
B. Project manager
C. Supplier assurance
D. Corporate, programme management or customer

Section: Organization Theme

QUESTION 36
Project Scenario – Health and Safety Training Project:

ABC Company is a well-established training company that uses a standard model to develop training materials and deliver courses to customers.

ABC Company has commissioned a project in response to recent changes in government legislation relating to health and safety on construction sites. The project will deliver "capability to provide health and safety training", including the materials needed for classroom-based training and e-learning. The expected benefits for construction companies include a reduction in lost days and legal costs due to accidents.

The e-learning course will be developed by a specialist external consultancy. The materials for classroom-based training will be delivered by ABC Company's development team. All course materials will be piloted before they are used. ABC Company will deliver training to its customers and also hopes to sell the course materials to other training companies as part of their operational business. ABC Company will use their own sales and marketing departments to promote the courses.

The legislation requires construction companies to comply with the new legislation within two years. The course materials and trainers have to be accredited by a government agency before courses can be delivered. ABC Company is planning to deliver pilot courses within five months of starting the project.

The ABC Company standard development model for new courses recommends the following stages:

End of the Project scenario.

Additional Information:

The Chief Executive Officer (CEO) founded the company five years ago. Under her leadership, ABC Company has grown quickly into a successful training company. It delivers a range of accredited professional training.

The Finance Director is also a founder member of ABC Company and is responsible for authorizing budgets for the Operations and Development Teams. She authorizes all large contracts personally.

The Purchasing Manager reports to the Finance Director and is responsible for managing and monitoring supplier contracts.

The Operations Director is responsible for the delivery off all training and for the training development budget. His department organizes courses, venues and trainers. They work with the Product and the Sales teams to provide a comprehensive training schedule. ABC Company's IT manager reports to the Operations Director.

The Business Development Director has recently been appointed to identify new training needs and propose new products. She will work with the Operations. Director to ensure a cost-conscious approach and that appropriate development technologies are used for the health and safety course.

The Training Development Manager reports to the Business Development Director and is responsible for developing training materials and gaining accreditation, in accordance with the standard course development model. Course developers in his team have skills in a range of development technologies and are allocated to projects as needed.

The Training Delivery Manager, who reports to the Operations Director, is responsible for ensuring that internal and external trainers deliver ABC Company training courses to the required standard. He also checks course materials to ensure they are fit for purpose and of the required quality.

The Central Services Director has responsibility for corporate communications, facilities management and configuration management. He recently led a project to consolidate all company quality systems into one quality management system and set up a corporate quality department, now managed by the Corporate Quality Manager.

The Corporate Document Manager reports to the Central Services Director. She helped establish the company's document management system and now operates

it across the business. She manages a team of administrators and contracts staff when workload is high.

The Sales Director joined ABC Company two months ago and is keen to establish himself by suggesting new markets for the courses and material. All account managers and the marketing team report to him. They promote existing training courses to other training companies and existing customers.

End of the additional information.
The project is at the end of stage 4. The project manager has changed the benefits management approach. It now includes all the activities necessary to measure the increased revenue.
Who should approve this update?

A. Corporate management
B. Project board
C. Project assurance
D. Project manager

Section: Organization Theme

QUESTION 37
Which principle is central to the quality theme and provides explicit understanding of what the project will create?

A. Manage by stages
B. Focus on products
C. Manage by exception
D. Learn from experience

Section: Quality Theme

QUESTION 38
Which of the following statements are True:

1. Quality management is the complete set of quality standards, procedures and responsibilities for a site or organization.
2. Quality planning is about defining products required of the project with their respective quality criteria, methods and responsibilities.
3. Quality control focuses on the operational techniques and activities used to carry out quality inspections
4. Quality assurance ensures that quality methods are being correctly followed.

A. 1, 2 & 3
B. 1, 3 & 4
C. 1, 2 & 4
D. 2, 3 & 4

Section: Quality Theme

QUESTION 39
In the PRINCE2 Quality review technique, who would most likely carry out the role of administrator:

A. Project manager
B. Project support
C. Team Manager
D. Project Assurance

Section: Quality Theme

QUESTION 40
Which role is responsible for providing the customer's quality expectations and acceptance criteria for the project?

A. Executive
B. Corporate or Programme Management
C. Senior User
D. Project Assurance

Section: Quality Theme

QUESTION 41
Which management product defines the detailed nature, purpose and function of a product?
A. Plan
B. Quality Register
C. Project Product Description
D. Product Description
Section: Quality Theme

QUESTION 42
HOTSPOT
Extract from the Project Product Description (with errors)

Composition	1. Monthly calendar displays
	2. 100gsm glossy paper
	3. Full colour
	4. Selected envelope
	5. Chosen label design
	6. List of customers
	7. Selected photos
	8. Photo session schedule
Derivation	9. New company logo design
	10. Previous calendar designs
	11. Internal creative team
	12. Production cost forecast
Development skills required	13. Photographer
	14. Internal creative team
	15. Printer
Customer's quality expectations	16. Professional photos
	17. 10% more calendars should be printed than required to allow for any late additions to the list of customers
	18. Compliance with applicable corporate standards
	19. The calendar should reflect the company image as described in the corporate branding standards
	20. The calendar will increase orders by at least 10% with a minimum of 10 further orders from the list of prospective customers within 12 months
Acceptance criteria	21. Appearance - each photo should be sufficiently attractive and humorous that the customer wants to display it
	22. Appearance - new company logo promotes strong image
	23. Security - complies with Data Protection Act
	24. Accuracy - public holidays match the list supplied by Marketing on 01 November

Column 1 is a list of objectives. For each objective in Column 1, select from Column 2 the quality activity that addresses it. Each selection from Column 2 can be used once, more than once or not at all. Drop down the right answer.

Hot

Column 1	Column 2
Understanding the customer's quality expectations.	Quality assurance / Quality control / Quality planning
Approval of the project's products.	Quality assurance / Quality control / Quality planning
Confirmation that corporate management standards and policies are being adhered to.	Quality assurance / Quality control / Quality planning

Section: Quality Theme
QUESTION 43
Scenario
Extract from the Project Product Description (with errors)

Composition	1. Monthly calendar displays 2. 100gsm glossy paper 3. Full colour 4. Selected envelope 5. Chosen label design 6. List of customers 7. Selected photos 8. Photo session schedule
Derivation	9. New company logo design 10. Previous calendar designs 11. Internal creative team 12. Production cost forecast
Development skills required	13. Photographer 14. Internal creative team 15. Printer
Customer's quality expectations	16. Professional photos 17. 10% more calendars should be printed than required to allow for any late additions to the list of customers 18. Compliance with applicable corporate standards 19. The calendar should reflect the company image as described in the corporate branding standards 20. The calendar will increase orders by at least 10% with a minimum of 10 further orders from the list of prospective customers within 12 months
Acceptance criteria	21. Appearance - each photo should be sufficiently attractive and humorous that the customer wants to display it 22. Appearance - new company logo promotes strong image 23. Security - complies with Data Protection Act 24. Accuracy - public holidays match the list supplied by Marketing on 01 November

Which 2 statements apply to the Composition section?

A. Amend entry 2 to 'Selected paper'.
B. Delete entry 3 because this is NOT a major product to be delivered by this project.
C. Move entry 6 to Derivation because this product already exists.
D. Delete entry 7 because these will be produced by the photographer.
E. Add 'Calendars distributed to customers'.

Section: Quality Theme

QUESTION 44
Scenario
Extract from the Project Product Description (with errors)

Composition	1. Monthly calendar displays 2. 100gsm glossy paper 3. Full colour 4. Selected envelope 5. Chosen label design 6. List of customers 7. Selected photos 8. Photo session schedule
Derivation	9. New company logo design 10. Previous calendar designs 11. Internal creative team 12. Production cost forecast
Development skills required	13. Photographer 14. Internal creative team 15. Printer
Customer's quality expectations	16. Professional photos 17. 10% more calendars should be printed than required to allow for any late additions to the list of customers 18. Compliance with applicable corporate standards 19. The calendar should reflect the company image as described in the corporate branding standards 20. The calendar will increase orders by at least 10% with a minimum of 10 further orders from the list of prospective customers within 12 months
Acceptance criteria	21. Appearance - each photo should be sufficiently attractive and humorous that the customer wants to display it 22. Appearance - new company logo promotes strong image 23. Security - complies with Data Protection Act 24. Accuracy - public holidays match the list supplied by Marketing on 01 November

Which 2 statements apply to the Derivation section?

A. Move entry 9 to Composition because this is within the scope of the project.
B. Delete entry 10 because this is NOT a source product for this project.
C. Delete entry 11 as this is already correctly shown under Development Skills required.
D. Move entry 12 to Composition, because this is within the scope of this project.
E. Add 'Professional photographer'.

Section: Quality Theme

QUESTION 45
Scenario
Extract from the Project Product Description (with errors)

Composition	1. Monthly calendar displays 2. 100gsm glossy paper 3. Full colour 4. Selected envelope 5. Chosen label design 6. List of customers 7. Selected photos 8. Photo session schedule
Derivation	9. New company logo design 10. Previous calendar designs 11. Internal creative team 12. Production cost forecast
Development skills required	13. Photographer 14. Internal creative team 15. Printer
Customer's quality expectations	16. Professional photos 17. 10% more calendars should be printed than required to allow for any late additions to the list of customers 18. Compliance with applicable corporate standards 19. The calendar should reflect the company image as described in the corporate branding standards 20. The calendar will increase orders by at least 10% with a minimum of 10 further orders from the list of prospective customers within 12 months
Acceptance criteria	21. Appearance - each photo should be sufficiently attractive and humorous that the customer wants to display it 22. Appearance - new company logo promotes strong image 23. Security - complies with Data Protection Act 24. Accuracy - public holidays match the list supplied by Marketing on 01 November

Which 2 statements apply to the Development skills required section?

A. Move entry 13 to Composition because the appointment of the photographer is within the scope of this project.

B. Move entry 13 to Derivation because this is a source of information for this project.
C. Delete entry 14 because this skill is NOT required within this project.
D. Delete entry 15 because this skill is NOT required within this project.
E. Add 'Knowledge of Data Protection Act.

Section: Quality Theme

QUESTION 46
Scenario
Extract from the Project Product Description (with errors)

Composition	1. Monthly calendar displays 2. 100gsm glossy paper 3. Full colour 4. Selected envelope 5. Chosen label design 6. List of customers 7. Selected photos 8. Photo session schedule
Derivation	9. New company logo design 10. Previous calendar designs 11. Internal creative team 12. Production cost forecast
Development skills required	13. Photographer 14. Internal creative team 15. Printer
Customer's quality expectations	16. Professional photos 17. 10% more calendars should be printed than required to allow for any late additions to the list of customers 18. Compliance with applicable corporate standards 19. The calendar should reflect the company image as described in the corporate branding standards 20. The calendar will increase orders by at least 10% with a minimum of 10 further orders from the list of prospective customers within 12 months
Acceptance criteria	21. Appearance - each photo should be sufficiently attractive and humorous that the customer wants to display it 22. Appearance - new company logo promotes strong image 23. Security - complies with Data Protection Act 24. Accuracy - public holidays match the list supplied by Marketing on 01 November

Which 2 statements apply to the Customer's quality expectations section?

A. Delete entry 16 because this should be shown on the Product Description for the photos.
B. Delete entry 17 because this is beyond the scope of this project.

C. Delete entry 18 because standards should NOT be shown here.
D. Delete entry 19 because this should appear in the Product Description for the calendar and not the Project Product Description.
E. Delete entry 20 because this is an expected benefit and should be recorded in the Business Case.

Section: Quality Theme

QUESTION 47
Scenario
Extract from the Project Product Description (with errors)

Composition	1. Monthly calendar displays 2. 100gsm glossy paper 3. Full colour 4. Selected envelope 5. Chosen label design 6. List of customers 7. Selected photos 8. Photo session schedule
Derivation	9. New company logo design 10. Previous calendar designs 11. Internal creative team 12. Production cost forecast
Development skills required	13. Photographer 14. Internal creative team 15. Printer
Customer's quality expectations	16. Professional photos 17. 10% more calendars should be printed than required to allow for any late additions to the list of customers 18. Compliance with applicable corporate standards 19. The calendar should reflect the company image as described in the corporate branding standards 20. The calendar will increase orders by at least 10% with a minimum of 10 further orders from the list of prospective customers within 12 months
Acceptance criteria	21. Appearance - each photo should be sufficiently attractive and humorous that the customer wants to display it 22. Appearance - new company logo promotes strong image 23. Security - complies with Data Protection Act 24. Accuracy - public holidays match the list supplied by Marketing on 01 November

Which 2 statements apply to the Acceptance criteria section?

A. Amend entry 21 to 'Appearance - 12 photos each showing different members of staff.
B. Move entry 21 to Composition because the photos are part of the final product.
C. Delete entry 22 because the development of the new company logo is not

within the scope of the Calendar project.
D. Move entry 23 to Derivation because the Data Protection Act already exists.
E. Delete entry 24 because this is NOT a suitable acceptance criteria for this project.

Section: Quality Theme

QUESTION 48
Scenario
Additional Information Product Description

Title	Service Level Agreement.
Purpose	• This agreement specifies the level of service MFH requires from the selected service provider and provides measurable criteria against which the selected service provider's performance will be assessed.
Composition	• Responsibilities of MFH and selected service provider. • Mechanisms for monitoring and reporting performance levels. • Dispute resolution process. • Confidentiality provisions. • Conditions for termination of contract. • Glossary of technical terms contained in SLA.
Format and presentation	• A4, Word document, printed both sides in black and white. • Font: Arial, 12pts.
Quality criteria	• Contains all composition items listed above. • Not more than 60 pages. • Complies with MFH corporate branding standards. • No typographical errors.
Quality skills required	• Proof-reading skills. • Director of Compliance Division - Reviewer. • Director of Information Technology Division - Reviewer. • Administrator.
Quality responsibilities	• Producer/Presenter: Director of Facilities Division. • Chair: Project Manager.

Quality notes from the Daily Log
The Director of Information Technology Division (DIT) has been asked to ensure that any changes to the outsourced staff employment contracts adhere to employment law. The DIT will review future job descriptions of the transferred staff before the final contract is signed with the selected service provider.

The service level agreement between MFH and the selected service provider will specify the type and quality of service required. The selected service provider must follow the industry standards for providing outsourced services.

MFH has a quality management system which contains a document control procedure for all its documentation, however this does not include change management.

All project documents will be subject to a quality review. Nominated products will require a formal approval record signed-off by the quality review chair. Extract from the draft Quality Management Strategy (may contain errors)
Introduction
1. This document defines the approach to be taken to achieve the required quality levels during the project.
2. The Project Board will have overall responsibility for the Quality Management Strategy.
3. Project Assurance will provide assurance on the implementation of the Quality Management Strategy. Quality management procedure - Quality standards
4. The selected service provider will operate to industry standards for providing outsourced services.
5. MFH document standards will be used.

Records
6. A Quality Register will be maintained to record the planned quality events and the actual results from the quality activities.
7. Configuration Item Records will be maintained for each product to describe its status, version and variant.
8. Approval records for products that require them will be stored in the quality database. Roles and responsibilities
9. The DIT will check that the employment contracts for outsourced staff adhere to employment law.
10. Team Managers will provide details of quality checks that have been carried out.
11. Team Managers will ensure that the Quality Register is updated with the names of team members who are involved in the review process.
12. The Senior User will review the Product Descriptions of the products to be produced by the selected service provider to ensure that they can be achieved.

Which is a correctly defined acceptance criterion for the service level agreement (SLA) with the selected service provider?

A. The SLA must extend for the full duration of the service contract.
B. Any changes to the SLA must be managed through formal change control.
C. External consultants are to assist in the creation of the SLA.
D. The selected service provider should be located locally.

Section: Quality Theme

QUESTION 49
Scenario
Additional Information Product Description

Title	Service Level Agreement.
Purpose	• This agreement specifies the level of service MFH requires from the selected service provider and provides measurable criteria against which the selected service provider's performance will be assessed.
Composition	• Responsibilities of MFH and selected service provider. • Mechanisms for monitoring and reporting performance levels. • Dispute resolution process. • Confidentiality provisions. • Conditions for termination of contract. • Glossary of technical terms contained in SLA.
Format and presentation	• A4, Word document, printed both sides in black and white. • Font: Arial, 12pts.
Quality criteria	• Contains all composition items listed above. • Not more than 60 pages. • Complies with MFH corporate branding standards. • No typographical errors.
Quality skills required	• Proof-reading skills. • Director of Compliance Division - Reviewer. • Director of Information Technology Division - Reviewer. • Administrator.
Quality responsibilities	• Producer/Presenter: Director of Facilities Division. • Chair: Project Manager.

Quality notes from the Daily Log

The Director of Information Technology Division (DIT) has been asked to ensure that any changes to the outsourced staff employment contracts adhere to employment law. The DIT will review future job descriptions of the transferred staff before the final contract is signed with the selected service provider.

The service level agreement between MFH and the selected service provider will specify the type and quality of service required. The selected service provider must follow the industry standards for providing outsourced services.

MFH has a quality management system which contains a document control procedure for all its documentation, however this does not include change management.

All project documents will be subject to a quality review. Nominated products will require a formal approval record signed-off by the quality review chair. Extract from the draft Quality Management Strategy (may contain errors)

Introduction
1. This document defines the approach to be taken to achieve the required quality levels during the project.
2. The Project Board will have overall responsibility for the Quality Management Strategy.
3. Project Assurance will provide assurance on the implementation of the Quality Management Strategy. Quality management procedure - Quality standards
4. The selected service provider will operate to industry standards for providing outsourced services.
5. MFH document standards will be used.

Records
6. A Quality Register will be maintained to record the planned quality events and the actual results from the quality activities.
7. Configuration Item Records will be maintained for each product to describe its status, version and variant.
8. Approval records for products that require them will be stored in the quality database. Roles and responsibilities
9. The DIT will check that the employment contracts for outsourced staff adhere to employment law.
10. Team Managers will provide details of quality checks that have been carried out.
11. Team Managers will ensure that the Quality Register is updated with the names of team members who are involved in the review process.
12. The Senior User will review the Product Descriptions of the products to be produced by the selected service provider to ensure that they can be achieved.

Which is a correctly defined acceptance criterion for the transferred facilities computer system?

A. Must be subject to regular back-ups.
B. Planned periods of shutdowns of the computer system must be kept to a minimum.
C. No (zero) loss of system functionality.
D. Back-up of data must be kept until the data is no longer needed.

Section: Quality Theme

QUESTION 50
Scenario
Additional Information Product Description

Title	Service Level Agreement.
Purpose	• This agreement specifies the level of service MFH requires from the selected service provider and provides measurable criteria against which the selected service provider's performance will be assessed.
Composition	• Responsibilities of MFH and selected service provider. • Mechanisms for monitoring and reporting performance levels. • Dispute resolution process. • Confidentiality provisions. • Conditions for termination of contract. • Glossary of technical terms contained in SLA.
Format and presentation	• A4, Word document, printed both sides in black and white. • Font: Arial, 12pts.
Quality criteria	• Contains all composition items listed above. • Not more than 60 pages. • Complies with MFH corporate branding standards. • No typographical errors.
Quality skills required	• Proof-reading skills. • Director of Compliance Division - Reviewer. • Director of Information Technology Division - Reviewer. • Administrator.
Quality responsibilities	• Producer/Presenter: Director of Facilities Division. • Chair: Project Manager.

Quality notes from the Daily Log

The Director of Information Technology Division (DIT) has been asked to ensure that any changes to the outsourced staff employment contracts adhere to employment law. The DIT will review future job descriptions of the transferred staff before the final contract is signed with the selected service provider.

The service level agreement between MFH and the selected service provider will specify the type and quality of service required. The selected service provider must follow the industry standards for providing outsourced services.

MFH has a quality management system which contains a document control procedure for all its documentation, however this does not include change management.

All project documents will be subject to a quality review. Nominated products will require a formal approval record signed-off by the quality review chair. Extract from the draft Quality Management Strategy (may contain errors)
Introduction
1. This document defines the approach to be taken to achieve the required quality levels during the project.
2. The Project Board will have overall responsibility for the Quality Management Strategy.
3. Project Assurance will provide assurance on the implementation of the Quality Management Strategy. Quality management procedure - Quality standards
4. The selected service provider will operate to industry standards for providing outsourced services.
5. MFH document standards will be used.

Records
6. A Quality Register will be maintained to record the planned quality events and the actual results from the quality activities.
7. Configuration Item Records will be maintained for each product to describe its status, version and variant.
8. Approval records for products that require them will be stored in the quality database. Roles and responsibilities
9. The DIT will check that the employment contracts for outsourced staff adhere to employment law.
10. Team Managers will provide details of quality checks that have been carried out.
11. Team Managers will ensure that the Quality Register is updated with the names of team members who are involved in the review process.
12. The Senior User will review the Product Descriptions of the products to be produced by the selected service provider to ensure that they can be achieved.

Which is a correctly defined acceptance criterion for the transferred staff?

A. No staff are to be left behind.
B. Staff should be transferred as soon as possible.
C. All legal requirements are adhered to for the transfer of staff.
D. Retained staff should be of reasonable competence to maintain the SLA.

Section: Quality Theme

QUESTION 51
Scenario
Additional Information Product Description

Title	Service Level Agreement.
Purpose	• This agreement specifies the level of service MFH requires from the selected service provider and provides measurable criteria against which the selected service provider's performance will be assessed.
Composition	• Responsibilities of MFH and selected service provider. • Mechanisms for monitoring and reporting performance levels. • Dispute resolution process. • Confidentiality provisions. • Conditions for termination of contract. • Glossary of technical terms contained in SLA.
Format and presentation	• A4, Word document, printed both sides in black and white. • Font: Arial, 12pts.
Quality criteria	• Contains all composition items listed above. • Not more than 60 pages. • Complies with MFH corporate branding standards. • No typographical errors.
Quality skills required	• Proof-reading skills. • Director of Compliance Division - Reviewer. • Director of Information Technology Division - Reviewer. • Administrator.
Quality responsibilities	• Producer/Presenter: Director of Facilities Division. • Chair: Project Manager.

Quality notes from the Daily Log
The Director of Information Technology Division (DIT) has been asked to ensure that any changes to the outsourced staff employment contracts adhere to employment law. The DIT will review future job descriptions of the transferred staff before the final contract is signed with the selected service provider.

The service level agreement between MFH and the selected service provider will specify the type and quality of service required. The selected service provider must follow the industry standards for providing outsourced services.

MFH has a quality management system which contains a document control procedure for all its documentation, however this does not include change management.

All project documents will be subject to a quality review. Nominated products will require a formal approval record signed-off by the quality review chair. Extract from the draft Quality Management Strategy (may contain errors)

Introduction
1. This document defines the approach to be taken to achieve the required quality levels during the project.
2. The Project Board will have overall responsibility for the Quality Management Strategy.
3. Project Assurance will provide assurance on the implementation of the Quality Management Strategy. Quality management procedure - Quality standards
4. The selected service provider will operate to industry standards for providing outsourced services.
5. MFH document standards will be used.

Records
6. A Quality Register will be maintained to record the planned quality events and the actual results from the quality activities.
7. Configuration Item Records will be maintained for each product to describe its status, version and variant.
8. Approval records for products that require them will be stored in the quality database. Roles and responsibilities
9. The DIT will check that the employment contracts for outsourced staff adhere to employment law.
10. Team Managers will provide details of quality checks that have been carried out.
11. Team Managers will ensure that the Quality Register is updated with the names of team members who are involved in the review process.
12. The Senior User will review the Product Descriptions of the products to be produced by the selected service provider to ensure that they can be achieved.

Which is a correctly defined acceptance criterion for the running cost of the outsourced service?

A. Must be kept to a minimum.
B. Must be kept to a level acceptable to the Ministry of Food Hygiene.
C. Subject to market conditions.
D. The annual increase to be less than half the rate of inflation.

Section: Quality Theme

QUESTION 52
Scenario
Additional Information Product Description

Title	Service Level Agreement.
Purpose	• This agreement specifies the level of service MFH requires from the selected service provider and provides measurable criteria against which the selected service provider's performance will be assessed.
Composition	• Responsibilities of MFH and selected service provider. • Mechanisms for monitoring and reporting performance levels. • Dispute resolution process. • Confidentiality provisions. • Conditions for termination of contract. • Glossary of technical terms contained in SLA.
Format and presentation	• A4, Word document, printed both sides in black and white. • Font: Arial, 12pts.
Quality criteria	• Contains all composition items listed above. • Not more than 60 pages. • Complies with MFH corporate branding standards. • No typographical errors.
Quality skills required	• Proof-reading skills. • Director of Compliance Division - Reviewer. • Director of Information Technology Division - Reviewer. • Administrator.
Quality responsibilities	• Producer/Presenter: Director of Facilities Division. • Chair: Project Manager.

Quality notes from the Daily Log

The Director of Information Technology Division (DIT) has been asked to ensure that any changes to the outsourced staff employment contracts adhere to employment law. The DIT will review future job descriptions of the transferred staff before the final contract is signed with the selected service provider.

The service level agreement between MFH and the selected service provider will specify the type and quality of service required. The selected service provider must follow the industry standards for providing outsourced services.

MFH has a quality management system which contains a document control procedure for all its documentation, however this does not include change management.
All project documents will be subject to a quality review. Nominated products will

require a formal approval record signed-off by the quality review chair. Extract from the draft Quality Management Strategy (may contain errors)

Introduction
1. This document defines the approach to be taken to achieve the required quality levels during the project.
2. The Project Board will have overall responsibility for the Quality Management Strategy.
3. Project Assurance will provide assurance on the implementation of the Quality Management Strategy. Quality management procedure - Quality standards
4. The selected service provider will operate to industry standards for providing outsourced services.
5. MFH document standards will be used.

Records
6. A Quality Register will be maintained to record the planned quality events and the actual results from the quality activities.
7. Configuration Item Records will be maintained for each product to describe its status, version and variant.
8. Approval records for products that require them will be stored in the quality database. Roles and responsibilities
9. The DIT will check that the employment contracts for outsourced staff adhere to employment law.
10. Team Managers will provide details of quality checks that have been carried out.
11. Team Managers will ensure that the Quality Register is updated with the names of team members who are involved in the review process.
12. The Senior User will review the Product Descriptions of the products to be produced by the selected service provider to ensure that they can be achieved.

Although it is not specified in the current corporate branding standards, the MFH corporate logo should be shown on the front page of the service level agreement.

A. Obtain agreement from the Director of Facilities Division to amend this within the remaining +2 days tolerance.
B. Raise an issue (off-specification).
C. Raise an issue (request for change).
D. Accept this error as a concession.

Section: Quality Theme

QUESTION 53
Scenario
Additional Information Product Description

Title	Service Level Agreement.
Purpose	• This agreement specifies the level of service MFH requires from the selected service provider and provides measurable criteria against which the selected service provider's performance will be assessed.
Composition	• Responsibilities of MFH and selected service provider. • Mechanisms for monitoring and reporting performance levels. • Dispute resolution process. • Confidentiality provisions. • Conditions for termination of contract. • Glossary of technical terms contained in SLA.
Format and presentation	• A4, Word document, printed both sides in black and white. • Font: Arial, 12pts.
Quality criteria	• Contains all composition items listed above. • Not more than 60 pages. • Complies with MFH corporate branding standards. • No typographical errors.
Quality skills required	• Proof-reading skills. • Director of Compliance Division - Reviewer. • Director of Information Technology Division - Reviewer. • Administrator.
Quality responsibilities	• Producer/Presenter: Director of Facilities Division. • Chair: Project Manager.

Quality notes from the Daily Log

The Director of Information Technology Division (DIT) has been asked to ensure that any changes to the outsourced staff employment contracts adhere to employment law. The DIT will review future job descriptions of the transferred staff before the final contract is signed with the selected service provider.

The service level agreement between MFH and the selected service provider will specify the type and quality of service required. The selected service provider must follow the industry standards for providing outsourced services.

MFH has a quality management system which contains a document control procedure for all its documentation, however this does not include change management.

All project documents will be subject to a quality review. Nominated products will require a formal approval record signed-off by the quality review chair. Extract from the draft Quality Management Strategy (may contain errors)

Introduction
1. This document defines the approach to be taken to achieve the required quality levels during the project.
2. The Project Board will have overall responsibility for the Quality Management Strategy.
3. Project Assurance will provide assurance on the implementation of the Quality Management Strategy. Quality management procedure - Quality standards
4. The selected service provider will operate to industry standards for providing outsourced services.
5. MFH document standards will be used.

Records
6. A Quality Register will be maintained to record the planned quality events and the actual results from the quality activities.
7. Configuration Item Records will be maintained for each product to describe its status, version and variant.
8. Approval records for products that require them will be stored in the quality database. Roles and responsibilities
9. The DIT will check that the employment contracts for outsourced staff adhere to employment law.
10. Team Managers will provide details of quality checks that have been carried out.
11. Team Managers will ensure that the Quality Register is updated with the names of team members who are involved in the review process.
12. The Senior User will review the Product Descriptions of the products to be produced by the selected service provider to ensure that they can be achieved.

The service level agreement looks like any other MFH document.

A. Obtain agreement from the Director of Facilities Division to redesign the service level agreement within the remaining +2 days tolerance.
B. Raise an issue (off-specification).
C. Accept this error as a concession.
D. No action required.

Section: Quality Theme

QUESTION 54
Scenario
Additional Information Product Description

Title	Service Level Agreement.
Purpose	• This agreement specifies the level of service MFH requires from the selected service provider and provides measurable criteria against which the selected service provider's performance will be assessed.
Composition	• Responsibilities of MFH and selected service provider. • Mechanisms for monitoring and reporting performance levels. • Dispute resolution process. • Confidentiality provisions. • Conditions for termination of contract. • Glossary of technical terms contained in SLA.
Format and presentation	• A4, Word document, printed both sides in black and white. • Font: Arial, 12pts.
Quality criteria	• Contains all composition items listed above. • Not more than 60 pages. • Complies with MFH corporate branding standards. • No typographical errors.
Quality skills required	• Proof-reading skills. • Director of Compliance Division - Reviewer. • Director of Information Technology Division - Reviewer. • Administrator.
Quality responsibilities	• Producer/Presenter: Director of Facilities Division. • Chair: Project Manager.

Quality notes from the Daily Log

The Director of Information Technology Division (DIT) has been asked to ensure that any changes to the outsourced staff employment contracts adhere to employment law. The DIT will review future job descriptions of the transferred staff before the final contract is signed with the selected service provider.

The service level agreement between MFH and the selected service provider will specify the type and quality of service required. The selected service provider must follow the industry standards for providing outsourced services.

MFH has a quality management system which contains a document control procedure for all its documentation, however this does not include change management.

All project documents will be subject to a quality review. Nominated products will require a formal approval record signed-off by the quality review chair. Extract from the draft Quality Management Strategy (may contain errors)

Introduction
1. This document defines the approach to be taken to achieve the required quality levels during the project.
2. The Project Board will have overall responsibility for the Quality Management Strategy.
3. Project Assurance will provide assurance on the implementation of the Quality Management Strategy. Quality management procedure - Quality standards
4. The selected service provider will operate to industry standards for providing outsourced services.
5. MFH document standards will be used.

Records
6. A Quality Register will be maintained to record the planned quality events and the actual results from the quality activities.
7. Configuration Item Records will be maintained for each product to describe its status, version and variant.
8. Approval records for products that require them will be stored in the quality database. Roles and responsibilities
9. The DIT will check that the employment contracts for outsourced staff adhere to employment law.
10. Team Managers will provide details of quality checks that have been carried out.
11. Team Managers will ensure that the Quality Register is updated with the names of team members who are involved in the review process.
12. The Senior User will review the Product Descriptions of the products to be produced by the selected service provider to ensure that they can be achieved.

The service level agreement contains a number of technical terms that are missing from its glossary of terms.

A. Obtain agreement from the Director of Facilities Division to add these into the glossary of terms within the remaining +2 days tolerance.
B. Raise an issue (off-specification).
C. Raise an issue (request for change).
D. No action required.

Section: Quality Theme

QUESTION 55
Scenario
Additional Information Product Description

Title	Service Level Agreement.
Purpose	• This agreement specifies the level of service MFH requires from the selected service provider and provides measurable criteria against which the selected service provider's performance will be assessed.
Composition	• Responsibilities of MFH and selected service provider. • Mechanisms for monitoring and reporting performance levels. • Dispute resolution process. • Confidentiality provisions. • Conditions for termination of contract. • Glossary of technical terms contained in SLA.
Format and presentation	• A4, Word document, printed both sides in black and white. • Font: Arial, 12pts.
Quality criteria	• Contains all composition items listed above. • Not more than 60 pages. • Complies with MFH corporate branding standards. • No typographical errors.
Quality skills required	• Proof-reading skills. • Director of Compliance Division - Reviewer. • Director of Information Technology Division - Reviewer. • Administrator.
Quality responsibilities	• Producer/Presenter: Director of Facilities Division. • Chair: Project Manager.

Quality notes from the Daily Log

The Director of Information Technology Division (DIT) has been asked to ensure that any changes to the outsourced staff employment contracts adhere to employment law. The DIT will review future job descriptions of the transferred staff before the final contract is signed with the selected service provider.

The service level agreement between MFH and the selected service provider will specify the type and quality of service required. The selected service provider must follow the industry standards for providing outsourced services.

MFH has a quality management system which contains a document control procedure for all its documentation, however this does not include change management.

All project documents will be subject to a quality review. Nominated products will require a formal approval record signed-off by the quality review chair. Extract from the draft Quality Management Strategy (may contain errors)

Introduction
1. This document defines the approach to be taken to achieve the required quality levels during the project.
2. The Project Board will have overall responsibility for the Quality Management Strategy.
3. Project Assurance will provide assurance on the implementation of the Quality Management Strategy. Quality management procedure - Quality standards
4. The selected service provider will operate to industry standards for providing outsourced services.
5. MFH document standards will be used.

Records
6. A Quality Register will be maintained to record the planned quality events and the actual results from the quality activities.
7. Configuration Item Records will be maintained for each product to describe its status, version and variant.
8. Approval records for products that require them will be stored in the quality database. Roles and responsibilities
9. The DIT will check that the employment contracts for outsourced staff adhere to employment law.
10. Team Managers will provide details of quality checks that have been carried out.
11. Team Managers will ensure that the Quality Register is updated with the names of team members who are involved in the review process.
12. The Senior User will review the Product Descriptions of the products to be produced by the selected service provider to ensure that they can be achieved.

Which statement applies to the Introduction section?

A. Delete entry 1 because the project approach is defined in the Project Brief.
B. Delete entry 2 because this is the Project Manager's responsibility.
C. Delete entry 3 because it is the Project Manager's responsibility to implement the Quality Management Strategy.
D. Move entry 3 to the Roles and responsibilities section because this is a quality responsibility.

Section: Quality Theme

QUESTION 56
Scenario
Additional Information Product Description

Title	Service Level Agreement.
Purpose	- This agreement specifies the level of service MFH requires from the selected service provider and provides measurable criteria against which the selected service provider's performance will be assessed.
Composition	- Responsibilities of MFH and selected service provider. - Mechanisms for monitoring and reporting performance levels. - Dispute resolution process. - Confidentiality provisions. - Conditions for termination of contract. - Glossary of technical terms contained in SLA.
Format and presentation	- A4, Word document, printed both sides in black and white. - Font: Arial, 12pts.
Quality criteria	- Contains all composition items listed above. - Not more than 60 pages. - Complies with MFH corporate branding standards. - No typographical errors.
Quality skills required	- Proof-reading skills. - Director of Compliance Division - Reviewer. - Director of Information Technology Division - Reviewer. - Administrator.
Quality responsibilities	- Producer/Presenter: Director of Facilities Division. - Chair: Project Manager.

Quality notes from the Daily Log

The Director of Information Technology Division (DIT) has been asked to ensure that any changes to the outsourced staff employment contracts adhere to employment law. The DIT will review future job descriptions of the transferred staff before the final contract is signed with the selected service provider.

The service level agreement between MFH and the selected service provider will specify the type and quality of service required. The selected service provider must follow the industry standards for providing outsourced services.

MFH has a quality management system which contains a document control procedure for all its documentation, however this does not include change management.

All project documents will be subject to a quality review. Nominated products will require a formal approval record signed-off by the quality review chair. Extract from the draft Quality Management Strategy (may contain errors)

Introduction
1. This document defines the approach to be taken to achieve the required quality levels during the project.
2. The Project Board will have overall responsibility for the Quality Management Strategy.
3. Project Assurance will provide assurance on the implementation of the Quality Management Strategy. Quality management procedure - Quality standards
4. The selected service provider will operate to industry standards for providing outsourced services.
5. MFH document standards will be used.

Records
6. A Quality Register will be maintained to record the planned quality events and the actual results from the quality activities.
7. Configuration Item Records will be maintained for each product to describe its status, version and variant.
8. Approval records for products that require them will be stored in the quality database. Roles and responsibilities
9. The DIT will check that the employment contracts for outsourced staff adhere to employment law.
10. Team Managers will provide details of quality checks that have been carried out.
11. Team Managers will ensure that the Quality Register is updated with the names of team members who are involved in the review process.
12. The Senior User will review the Product Descriptions of the products to be produced by the selected service provider to ensure that they can be achieved.

Which statement applies to the Quality standards section?

A. Delete entry 4 because external suppliers are responsible for applying any relevant standards to their work.
B. Delete entry 5 because the lack of a change management procedure makes the MFH document standards unsuitable.
C. Add 'All contracts must conform to current employment laws".
D. Add 'PRINCE2 change control procedures will be used to manage any changes to baselined products'.

Section: Quality Theme

QUESTION 57
Scenario
Additional Information Product Description

Title	Service Level Agreement.
Purpose	• This agreement specifies the level of service MFH requires from the selected service provider and provides measurable criteria against which the selected service provider's performance will be assessed.
Composition	• Responsibilities of MFH and selected service provider. • Mechanisms for monitoring and reporting performance levels. • Dispute resolution process. • Confidentiality provisions. • Conditions for termination of contract. • Glossary of technical terms contained in SLA.
Format and presentation	• A4, Word document, printed both sides in black and white. • Font: Arial, 12pts.
Quality criteria	• Contains all composition items listed above. • Not more than 60 pages. • Complies with MFH corporate branding standards. • No typographical errors.
Quality skills required	• Proof-reading skills. • Director of Compliance Division - Reviewer. • Director of Information Technology Division - Reviewer. • Administrator.
Quality responsibilities	• Producer/Presenter: Director of Facilities Division. • Chair: Project Manager.

Quality notes from the Daily Log
The Director of Information Technology Division (DIT) has been asked to ensure that any changes to the outsourced staff employment contracts adhere to employment law. The DIT will review future job descriptions of the transferred staff before the final contract is signed with the selected service provider.

The service level agreement between MFH and the selected service provider will specify the type and quality of service required. The selected service provider must follow the industry standards for providing outsourced services.
MFH has a quality management system which contains a document control procedure for all its documentation, however this does not include change management.

All project documents will be subject to a quality review. Nominated products will require a formal approval record signed-off by the quality review chair. Extract from the draft Quality Management Strategy (may contain errors)

Introduction
1. This document defines the approach to be taken to achieve the required quality levels during the project.
2. The Project Board will have overall responsibility for the Quality Management Strategy.
3. Project Assurance will provide assurance on the implementation of the Quality Management Strategy. Quality management procedure - Quality standards
4. The selected service provider will operate to industry standards for providing outsourced services.
5. MFH document standards will be used.

Records
6. A Quality Register will be maintained to record the planned quality events and the actual results from the quality activities.
7. Configuration Item Records will be maintained for each product to describe its status, version and variant.
8. Approval records for products that require them will be stored in the quality database. Roles and responsibilities
9. The DIT will check that the employment contracts for outsourced staff adhere to employment law.
10. Team Managers will provide details of quality checks that have been carried out.
11. Team Managers will ensure that the Quality Register is updated with the names of team members who are involved in the review process.
12. The Senior User will review the Product Descriptions of the products to be produced by the selected service provider to ensure that they can be achieved.

Which statement applies to the Records section?

A. Delete entry 6 because this information should be included in Stage or Team Plans.
B. Move entry 6 to the Reporting section because the information should be used to report on quality activities.
C. Delete entry 7 because this should be included in the Configuration Management Strategy.
D. Delete entry 8 because the results of quality reviews are recorded in the Quality Register.

Section: Quality Theme

QUESTION 58
Project Scenario – Health and Safety Training Project:

ABC Company is a well-established training company that uses a standard model to develop training materials and deliver courses to customers.

ABC Company has commissioned a project in response to recent changes in government legislation relating to health and safety on construction sites. The project will deliver "capability to provide health and safety training", including the materials needed for classroom-based training and e-learning. The expected benefits for construction companies include a reduction in lost days and legal costs due to accidents.

The e-learning course will be developed by a specialist external consultancy. The materials for classroom-based training will be delivered by ABC Company's development team. All course materials will be piloted before they are used. ABC Company will deliver training to its customers and also hopes to sell the course materials to other training companies as part of their operational business. ABC Company will use their own sales and marketing departments to promote the courses.

The legislation requires construction companies to comply with the new legislation within two years. The course materials and trainers have to be accredited by a government agency before courses can be delivered. ABC Company is planning to deliver pilot courses within five months of starting the project.

The ABC Company standard development model for new courses recommends the following stages:

End of the Project scenario.

Additional Information:

The <u>Chief Executive Officer (CEO)</u> founded the company five years ago. Under her leadership, ABC Company has grown quickly into a successful training company. It delivers a range of accredited professional training.

The <u>Finance Director</u> is also a founder member of ABC Company and is responsible for authorizing budgets for the Operations and Development Teams. She authorizes all large contracts personally.

The <u>Purchasing Manager</u> reports to the Finance Director and is responsible for managing and monitoring supplier contracts.

The <u>Operations Director</u> is responsible for the delivery off all training and for the

training development budget. His department organizes courses, venues and trainers. They work with the Product and the Sales teams to provide a comprehensive training schedule. ABC Company's IT manager reports to the Operations Director.

The <u>Business Development Director</u> has recently been appointed to identify new training needs and propose new products. She will work with the Operations. Director to ensure a cost-conscious approach and that appropriate development technologies are used for the health and safety course.

The <u>Training Development Manager</u> reports to the Business Development Director and is responsible for developing training materials and gaining accreditation, in

accordance with the standard course development model. Course developers in his team have skills in a range of development technologies and are allocated to projects as needed.

The <u>Training Delivery Manager</u>, who reports to the Operations Director, is responsible for ensuring that internal and external trainers deliver ABC Company training courses to the required standard. He also checks course materials to ensure they are fit for purpose and of the required quality.

The <u>Central Services Director</u> has responsibility for corporate communications, facilities management and configuration management. He recently led a project to consolidate all company quality systems into one quality management system and set up a corporate quality department, now managed by the Corporate Quality Manager.

The <u>Corporate Document Manager</u> reports to the Central Services Director. She helped establish the company's document management system and now operates it across the business. She manages a team of administrators and contracts staff when workload is high.

The <u>Sales Director</u> joined ABC Company two months ago and is keen to establish himself by suggesting new markets for the courses and material. All account managers and the marketing team report to him. They promote existing training courses to other training companies and existing customers.

End of the additional information.

A quality review of the 'marketing materials' has started. The team manager for the 'marketing materials' has been unhappy with the team's workload throughout the project and refuses to attend the review meeting to present the material. The team manager suggests that a new marketing team member make the presentation. However, the chair decides to represent the marketing team

and makes a list of actions to resolve later.
Is this an appropriate approach to the quality review, and why?

A. Yes, because the role of presenter should not be performed by a junior member of the team.
B. Yes, because the roles of chair, presenter and administrator may be combined.
C. No, because the role of presenter should be performed by the team manager.
D. No, because the chair should be independent from the product being reviewed.

Section: Quality Theme

QUESTION 59
Project Scenario – Health and Safety Training Project:

ABC Company is a well-established training company that uses a standard model to develop training materials and deliver courses to customers.

ABC Company has commissioned a project in response to recent changes in government legislation relating to health and safety on construction sites. The project

will deliver "capability to provide health and safety training", including the materials needed for classroom-based training and e-learning. The expected benefits for construction companies include a reduction in lost days and legal costs due to accidents.

The e-learning course will be developed by a specialist external consultancy. The materials for classroom-based training will be delivered by ABC Company's development team. All course materials will be piloted before they are used. ABC Company will deliver training to its customers and also hopes to sell the course materials to other training companies as part of their operational business. ABC Company will use their own sales and marketing departments to promote the courses.

The legislation requires construction companies to comply with the new legislation within two years. The course materials and trainers have to be accredited by a government agency before courses can be delivered. ABC Company is planning to deliver pilot courses within five months of starting the project.

The ABC Company standard development model for new courses recommends the following stages:

End of the Project scenario.

Additional Information:

The Chief Executive Officer (CEO) founded the company five years ago. Under her leadership, ABC Company has grown quickly into a successful training company. It delivers a range of accredited professional training.

The Finance Director is also a founder member of ABC Company and is responsible for authorizing budgets for the Operations and Development Teams. She authorizes all large contracts personally.

The Purchasing Manager reports to the Finance Director and is responsible for managing and monitoring supplier contracts.

The Operations Director is responsible for the delivery off all training and for the training development budget. His department organizes courses, venues and trainers. They work with the Product and the Sales teams to provide a comprehensive training schedule. ABC Company's IT manager reports to the Operations Director.

The Business Development Director has recently been appointed to identify new training needs and propose new products. She will work with the Operations. Director to ensure a cost-conscious approach and that appropriate development technologies are used for the health and safety course.

The Training Development Manager reports to the Business Development Director and is responsible for developing training materials and gaining accreditation, in accordance with the standard course development model. Course developers in his team have skills in a range of development technologies and are allocated to projects as needed.

The Training Delivery Manager, who reports to the Operations Director, is responsible for ensuring that internal and external trainers deliver ABC Company training courses to the required standard. He also checks course materials to ensure they are fit for purpose and of the required quality.

The Central Services Director has responsibility for corporate communications, facilities management and configuration management. He recently led a project to consolidate all company quality systems into one quality management system and set up a corporate quality department, now managed by the Corporate Quality Manager.

The Corporate Document Manager reports to the Central Services Director. She helped establish the company's document management system and now operates it across the business. She manages a team of administrators and contracts staff when workload is high.

The Sales Director joined ABC Company two months ago and is keen to establish himself by suggesting new markets for the courses and material. All account managers and the marketing team report to him. They promote existing training courses to other training companies and existing customers.

End of the additional information.

At the end of stage 2, the specialist 'e-learning course' supplier will be selected. As a result, it is decided that the quality management approach will not be created until the end of stage 2, to take into account this supplier's standards and techniques.
Is this appropriate, and why?

A. Yes, because the quality management approach should take into account the supplier's standards, tools and techniques.
B. Yes, because the product description for each product will define the required quality approach within each stage.
C. No, because the quality management approach should be created during the initiation stage and updated later.
D. No, because the quality management approach should be limited to ABC Company's quality standards.

Section: Quality Theme

QUESTION 60
PRINCE2 proposes 3 levels of Plan, which are they?

A. Initiation, Project and Stage Plans
B. Project, Stage and Exception Plans
C. Initiation, Project and Benefit Review Plans
D. Project, Stage and Team Plans

Section: Plans Theme

QUESTION 61
Having completed designing the plan, in which order should the next steps take place to produce a plan?
1. Prepare Estimates
2. Define and analyze Products
3. Prepare the schedule
4. Identify activities and dependencies

A. 2, 4, 3, 1
B. 4, 2, 1, 3
C. 4, 3, 2, 1
D. 2, 4, 1, 3

Section: Plans Theme

QUESTION 62
Product based planning focuses on which of the following:
1. Creating product descriptions
2. Identifying activities
3. Creating a Product hierarchy
4. Creating a Product sequence

A. 1, 2, 3
B. 2, 3, 4
C. 1, 3, 4
D. 1, 2, 4

Section: Plans Theme

QUESTION 63
Who sets the tolerances for a work package?

A. The project board
B. The project manager
C. The team manager
D. Corporate or programme management

Section: Plans Theme

QUESTION 64
Which of the following is not part of the composition of a Plan?

A. Pre-requites
B. Assumptions
C. Quality responsibilities
D. Product descriptions

Section: Plans Theme

QUESTION 65
Who is responsible for committing user resources to the project?

A. Senior User
B. Senior Supplier
C. Executive
D. Project Board

Section: Plans Theme

QUESTION 66
Scenario
Product Summary
A list of customers will be collated. This will use existing information from the Accounts department about current customers, and existing information from the Marketing department about prospective customers.

Using the tariff of mailing costs available from the Post Office, a production cost forecast will be produced to allow the CEO and the Marketing Director to decide whether to continue with the project. If they decide to continue, they will give the approval to launch the internal label design competition. Competition rules will be required to communicate details of the competition to the staff. The chosen label design will then be selected from the competition entries.
The photos for the calendar must be based on existing photo design ideas available from the Marketing department. The selected photos will be chosen from these. Monthly calendar displays will be created to show the required layout of each page.

Product Breakdown Structure (contains errors)

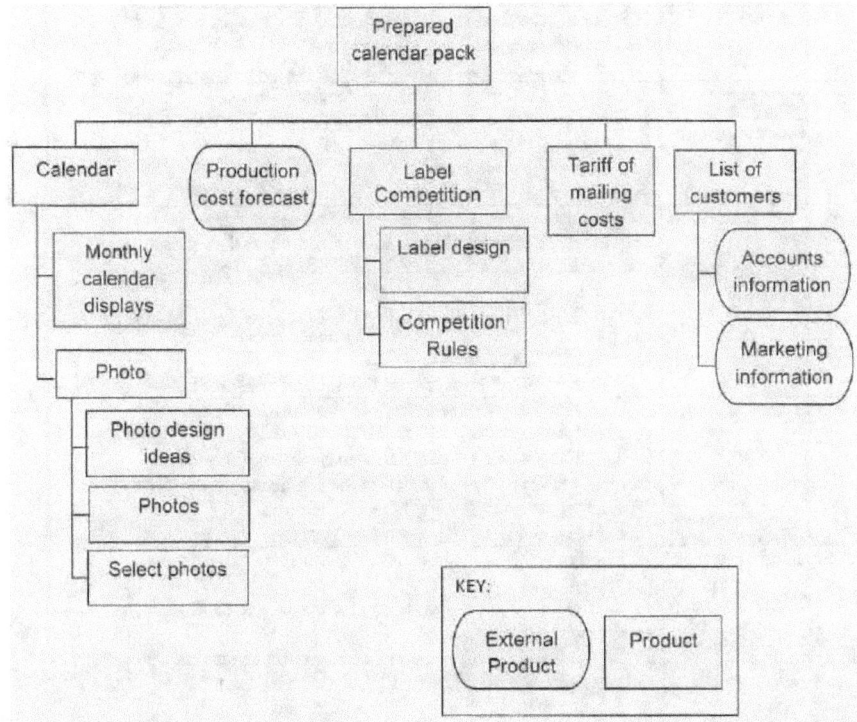

Extract from Stage Plan for stage 3.
(All entries are true statements but may not be shown under the correct heading or in the correct document).

Plan description	1. Stage 3 is the final stage of the project and will deliver the photos, the label design competition entries, the winning label design and the prepared calendar pack.
Plan prerequisites	2. Increase in orders and improved company image. 3. The production cost forecast must be acceptable to the Project Board if the photography and label design competition are to go ahead. 4. The customer list is accurate and complete.
External dependencies	5. A separate project has been reviewing the company's branding. The company logo, required for the label design competition, is being updated. The new company logo is to be supplied by the other project in two weeks time. 6. Customer details will be supplied from the Accounts department and the Marketing department customer databases for the customer list. 7. The label design must contain the new company logo.
Planning assumptions	8. A suitable entry will be received from the label design competition. 9. The photo session schedule created two weeks ago correctly reflects the availability of the engineering staff. 10. Each photo must feature different members of the Engineering team.
Monitoring and control	11. The Project Plan is to be updated with actual throughout the stage. 12. A Highlight Report will be created for the Project Board every two weeks. 13. The Stage Plan will be reviewed at the end of each day, to assess forecast against actual. 14. Product Status Accounts will be produced by Project Support, at the request of the Project Manager, to summarize current and historical data concerning each of the project's products.
Budgets	15. Cost £5k for specialist products 16. Time 4 weeks 17. Risk £0

Using the Project Scenario and the Extract from Stage Plan for stage 3 provided as additional intonation for this question in the Scenario Booklet, answer the following 5 questions.

The Stage Plan for stage 3 has been produced.

The Engineering Manager insists that there are to be no interruptions to operations whilst photographs are being taken of the engineering staff performing their everyday duties and operating machinery. Two weeks ago the professional photographer produced the photo session schedule based on the operational staff schedule. The operational staff schedule is produced weekly and maintained by the Engineering Manager.

None of the £500 change budget has been used to date and this is available for the stage. Which 2 statements apply to the Plan prerequisites section?

A. Delete entry 2 because these are project benefits not prerequisites of the stage.
B. Delete entry 3 because the production cost forecast is a deliverable of stage 2, not a prerequisite for stage 3.

C. Delete entry 4 because the customer list is a deliverable of stage 2, not a prerequisite for stage 3.
D. Add 'Engineering team must be made available for photos'.
E. Add 'Compliance with the Data Protection Act'.

Section: Plans Theme

QUESTION 67
Scenario
Product Summary

A list of customers will be collated. This will use existing information from the Accounts department about current customers, and existing information from the Marketing department about prospective customers.

Using the tariff of mailing costs available from the Post Office, a production cost forecast will be produced to allow the CEO and the Marketing Director to decide whether to continue with the project. If they decide to continue, they will give the approval to launch the internal label design competition. Competition rules will be required to communicate details of the competition to the staff. The chosen label design will then be selected from the competition entries.

The photos for the calendar must be based on existing photo design ideas available from the Marketing department. The selected photos will be chosen from these. Monthly calendar displays will be created to show the required layout of each page.

Product Breakdown Structure (contains errors)

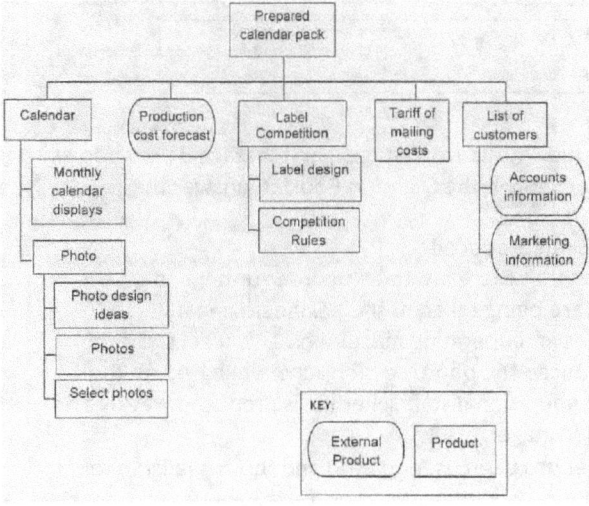

Extract from Stage Plan for stage 3.
(All entries are true statements but may not be shown under the correct heading

or in the correct document).

Plan description	1. Stage 3 is the final stage of the project and will deliver the photos, the label design competition entries, the winning label design and the prepared calendar pack.
Plan prerequisites	2. Increase in orders and improved company image. 3. The production cost forecast must be acceptable to the Project Board if the photography and label design competition are to go ahead. 4. The customer list is accurate and complete.
External dependencies	5. A separate project has been reviewing the company's branding. The company logo, required for the label design competition, is being updated. The new company logo is to be supplied by the other project in two weeks time. 6. Customer details will be supplied from the Accounts department and the Marketing department customer databases for the customer list. 7. The label design must contain the new company logo.
Planning assumptions	8. A suitable entry will be received from the label design competition. 9. The photo session schedule created two weeks ago correctly reflects the availability of the engineering staff. 10. Each photo must feature different members of the Engineering team.
Monitoring and control	11. The Project Plan is to be updated with actual throughout the stage. 12. A Highlight Report will be created for the Project Board every two weeks. 13. The Stage Plan will be reviewed at the end of each day, to assess forecast against actual. 14. Product Status Accounts will be produced by Project Support, at the request of the Project Manager, to summarize current and historical data concerning each of the project's products.
Budgets	15. Cost £5k for specialist products 16. Time 4 weeks 17. Risk £0

Using the Project Scenario and the Extract from Stage Plan for stage 3 provided as additional intonation for this question in the Scenario Booklet, answer the following 5 questions.
The Stage Plan for stage 3 has been produced.
The Engineering Manager insists that there are to be no interruptions to operations whilst photographs are being taken of the engineering staff performing their everyday duties and operating machinery. Two weeks ago the professional photographer produced the photo session schedule based on the operational staff schedule. The operational staff schedule is produced weekly and maintained by the Engineering Manager.
None of the £500 change budget has been used to date and this is available for

the stage. Which 2 statements apply to the Planning assumptions section?

A. No change to entry 8 because this cannot be confirmed until all of the label

designs entries have been received and an assessment made.
B. Move entry 8 to External dependencies because the label designs are created outside of the scope of the project.
C. Delete entry 9 because the photo session schedule should have been approved as part of stage 2.
D. Move entry 9 to External dependencies because the photo session schedule is created by the professional photographer.
E. Delete entry 10 because the inclusion of different members from the Engineering team in each photo should be shown in the Product Description for the photos.

Section: Plans Theme

QUESTION 68
Scenario
Product Summary
A list of customers will be collated. This will use existing information from the Accounts department about current customers, and existing information from the Marketing department about prospective customers.

Using the tariff of mailing costs available from the Post Office, a production cost forecast will be produced to allow the CEO and the Marketing Director to decide whether to continue with the project. If they decide to continue, they will give the approval to launch the internal label design competition. Competition rules will be required to communicate details of the competition to the staff. The chosen label design will then be selected from the competition entries.
The photos for the calendar must be based on existing photo design ideas available from the Marketing department. The selected photos will be chosen from these. Monthly calendar displays will be created to show the required layout of each page.

Product Breakdown Structure (contains errors)

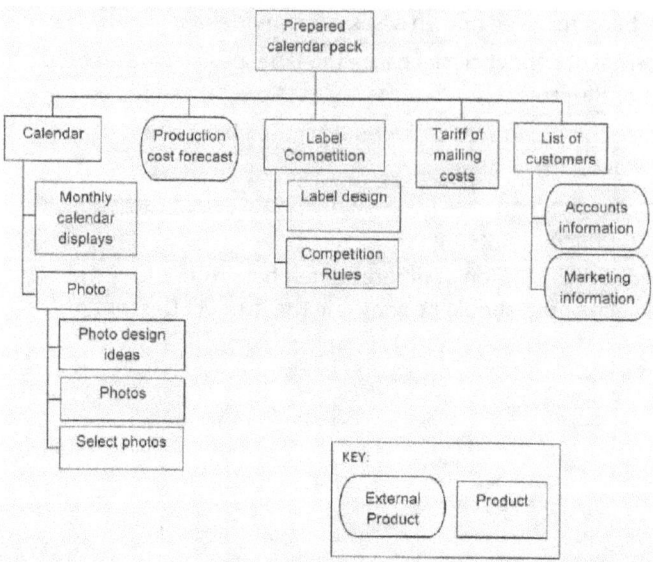

Extract from Stage Plan for stage 3.
(All entries are true statements but may not be shown under the correct heading or in the correct document).

Plan description	1. Stage 3 is the final stage of the project and will deliver the photos, the label design competition entries, the winning label design and the prepared calendar pack.
Plan prerequisites	2. Increase in orders and improved company image. 3. The production cost forecast must be acceptable to the Project Board if the photography and label design competition are to go ahead. 4. The customer list is accurate and complete.
External dependencies	5. A separate project has been reviewing the company's branding. The company logo, required for the label design competition, is being updated. The new company logo is to be supplied by the other project in two weeks time. 6. Customer details will be supplied from the Accounts department and the Marketing department customer databases for the customer list. 7. The label design must contain the new company logo.
Planning assumptions	8. A suitable entry will be received from the label design competition. 9. The photo session schedule created two weeks ago correctly reflects the availability of the engineering staff. 10. Each photo must feature different members of the Engineering team.
Monitoring and control	11. The Project Plan is to be updated with actual throughout the stage. 12. A Highlight Report will be created for the Project Board every two weeks. 13. The Stage Plan will be reviewed at the end of each day, to assess forecast against actual. 14. Product Status Accounts will be produced by Project Support, at the request of the Project Manager, to summarize current and historical data concerning each of the project's products.
Budgets	15. Cost £5k for specialist products 16. Time 4 weeks 17. Risk £0

Using the Project Scenario and the Extract from Stage Plan for stage 3 provided as additional intonation for this question in the Scenario Booklet, answer the following 5 questions.

The Stage Plan for stage 3 has been produced.

The Engineering Manager insists that there are to be no interruptions to operations whilst photographs are being taken of the engineering staff performing their everyday duties and operating machinery. Two weeks ago the professional photographer produced the photo session schedule based on the operational staff schedule. The operational staff schedule is produced weekly and maintained by the Engineering Manager.

None of the £500 change budget has been used to date and this is available for

the stage. Which 2 statements apply to the Budgets section?

A. Amend entry 15 because it should also include the cost of management activities.
B. Delete entry 16 because timescales should NOT be shown under the heading of budgets.
C. Delete entry 17 because the risk budget should be shown in the Risk Management Strategy.
D. Add 'Change budget - £500'.
E. Add 'Cost tolerance - +£6k 1-£6k

Section: Plans Theme

QUESTION 69
Project Scenario – Health and Safety Training Project:

ABC Company is a well-established training company that uses a standard model to develop training materials and deliver courses to customers.

ABC Company has commissioned a project in response to recent changes in government legislation relating to health and safety on construction sites. The project will deliver "capability to provide health and safety training", including the materials needed for classroom-based training and e-learning. The expected benefits for construction companies include a reduction in lost days and legal costs due to accidents.

The e-learning course will be developed by a specialist external consultancy. The materials for classroom-based training will be delivered by ABC Company's development team. All course materials will be piloted before they are used. ABC Company will deliver training to its customers and also hopes to sell the course materials to other training companies as part of their operational business. ABC

Company will use their own sales and marketing departments to promote the courses.

The legislation requires construction companies to comply with the new legislation within two years. The course materials and trainers have to be accredited by a government agency before courses can be delivered. ABC Company is planning to deliver pilot courses within five months of starting the project.

The ABC Company standard development model for new courses recommends the following stages:

Stage 1	Initiation stage
Stage 2	Classroom-based training materials Marketing materials Training venue specifications Accredited classroom-based course
Stage 3	E-learning course Amended course booking procedures Marketed courses Planned pilot courses Updated corporate quality procedures Accredited e-learning course Accredited trainers
Stage 4	Delivered pilot courses Finalized materials Project product: Capability to provide health and safety training

End of the Project scenario.

Additional Information:

The Chief Executive Officer (CEO) founded the company five years ago. Under her leadership, ABC Company has grown quickly into a successful training company. It delivers a range of accredited professional training.

The Finance Director is also a founder member of ABC Company and is responsible for authorizing budgets for the Operations and Development Teams. She authorizes all large contracts personally.

The Purchasing Manager reports to the Finance Director and is responsible for managing and monitoring supplier contracts.

The Operations Director is responsible for the delivery off all training and for the training development budget. His department organizes courses, venues and trainers. They work with the Product and the Sales teams to provide a comprehensive training schedule. ABC Company's IT manager reports to the

Operations Director.

The <u>Business Development Director</u> has recently been appointed to identify new training needs and propose new products. She will work with the Operations. Director to ensure a cost-conscious approach and that appropriate development technologies are used for the health and safety course.

The <u>Training Development Manager</u> reports to the Business Development Director and is responsible for developing training materials and gaining accreditation, in accordance with the standard course development model. Course developers in his team have skills in a range of development technologies and are allocated to projects as needed.

The <u>Training Delivery Manager</u>, who reports to the Operations Director, is responsible for ensuring that internal and external trainers deliver ABC Company training courses to the required standard. He also checks course materials to ensure they are fit for purpose and of the required quality.

The <u>Central Services Director</u> has responsibility for corporate communications, facilities management and configuration management. He recently led a project to consolidate all company quality systems into one quality management system and set up a corporate quality department, now managed by the Corporate Quality Manager.

The <u>Corporate Document Manager</u> reports to the Central Services Director. She helped establish the company's document management system and now operates it across the business. She manages a team of administrators and contracts staff when workload is high.

The <u>Sales Director</u> joined ABC Company two months ago and is keen to establish himself by suggesting new markets for the courses and material. All account managers and the marketing team report to him. They promote existing training courses to other training companies and existing customers.

End of the additional information.

In order for ABC Company to achieve the expected sales of the health and safety training course, the senior user will need to ensure that all staff understand the objectives and target audience for the course. In addition, these sales will need to be added to each individual's sales targets. These activities have been included in the benefits management approach.
Is this appropriate, and why?

A. Yes, because how the benefits will be measured needs to be documented.
B. Yes, because the actions required to achieve the outcomes need to be

documented.
C. No, because the expected sales increase should be recorded in the business case.
D. No, because actions to deliver the outputs should be recorded in the stage plan.

Section: Plans Theme

QUESTION 70
Project Scenario – Health and Safety Training Project:
ABC Company is a well-established training company that uses a standard model to develop training materials and deliver courses to customers.

ABC Company has commissioned a project in response to recent changes in government legislation relating to health and safety on construction sites. The project will deliver "capability to provide health and safety training", including the materials needed for classroom-based training and e-learning. The expected benefits for construction companies include a reduction in lost days and legal costs due to accidents.

The e-learning course will be developed by a specialist external consultancy. The materials for classroom-based training will be delivered by ABC Company's development team. All course materials will be piloted before they are used. ABC Company will deliver training to its customers and also hopes to sell the course materials to other training companies as part of their operational business. ABC Company will use their own sales and marketing departments to promote the courses.

The legislation requires construction companies to comply with the new legislation within two years. The course materials and trainers have to be accredited by a government agency before courses can be delivered. ABC Company is planning to deliver pilot courses within five months of starting the project.

The ABC Company standard development model for new courses recommends the following stages:

Stage 1	Initiation stage
Stage 2	Classroom-based training materials Marketing materials Training venue specifications Accredited classroom-based course
Stage 3	E-learning course Amended course booking procedures Marketed courses Planned pilot courses Updated corporate quality procedures Accredited e-learning course Accredited trainers
Stage 4	Delivered pilot courses Finalized materials Project product: Capability to provide health and safety training

End of the Project scenario.

Additional Information:

The <u>Chief Executive Officer (CEO)</u> founded the company five years ago. Under her leadership, ABC Company has grown quickly into a successful training company. It delivers a range of accredited professional training.

The <u>Finance Director</u> is also a founder member of ABC Company and is responsible for authorizing budgets for the Operations and Development Teams. She authorizes all large contracts personally.

The <u>Purchasing Manager</u> reports to the Finance Director and is responsible for managing and monitoring supplier contracts.

The <u>Operations Director</u> is responsible for the delivery off all training and for the training development budget. His department organizes courses, venues and trainers. They work with the Product and the Sales teams to provide a comprehensive training schedule. ABC Company's IT manager reports to the Operations Director.

The <u>Business Development Director</u> has recently been appointed to identify new training needs and propose new products. She will work with the Operations. Director to ensure a cost-conscious approach and that appropriate development technologies are used for the health and safety course.

The <u>Training Development Manager</u> reports to the Business Development Director and is responsible for developing training materials and gaining accreditation, in accordance with the standard course development model. Course developers in his team have skills in a range of development technologies and are allocated to projects as needed.

The <u>Training Delivery Manager</u>, who reports to the Operations Director, is responsible for ensuring that internal and external trainers deliver ABC Company training courses to the required standard. He also checks course materials to ensure they are fit for purpose and of the required quality.

The <u>Central Services Director</u> has responsibility for corporate communications, facilities management and configuration management. He recently led a project to consolidate all company quality systems into one quality management system and set up a corporate quality department, now managed by the Corporate Quality Manager.

The <u>Corporate Document Manager</u> reports to the Central Services Director. She

helped establish the company's document management system and now operates it across the business. She manages a team of administrators and contracts staff when workload is high.

The Sales Director joined ABC Company two months ago and is keen to establish himself by suggesting new markets for the courses and material. All account managers and the marketing team report to him. They promote existing training courses to other training companies and existing customers.

End of the additional information.

The executive identified that there would be a benefit to the construction companies as their working time lost due to accidents would be reduced. This was included as a benefit to ABC Company in the business case for the Health and Safety Training Project.
Is this appropriate, and why?

A. Yes, because the benefits to the customer are an essential part of business justification for a project.
B. Yes, because both tangible and intangible benefits should be included in the business case.
C. No, because ABC Company will not achieve their benefits if construction companies do not book the courses.
D. No, because it is the customer's benefits that should be used to justify the project business case.

Section: Plans Theme

QUESTION 71
Project Scenario – Health and Safety Training Project:

ABC Company is a well-established training company that uses a standard model to develop training materials and deliver courses to customers.

ABC Company has commissioned a project in response to recent changes in government legislation relating to health and safety on construction sites. The project will deliver "capability to provide health and safety training", including the materials needed for classroom-based training and e-learning. The expected benefits for construction companies include a reduction in lost days and legal costs due to accidents.

The e-learning course will be developed by a specialist external consultancy. The materials for classroom-based training will be delivered by ABC Company's development team. All course materials will be piloted before they are used. ABC

Company will deliver training to its customers and also hopes to sell the course materials to other training companies as part of their operational business. ABC Company will use their own sales and marketing departments to promote the courses.

The legislation requires construction companies to comply with the new legislation within two years. The course materials and trainers have to be accredited by a government agency before courses can be delivered. ABC Company is planning to deliver pilot courses within five months of starting the project.

The ABC Company standard development model for new courses recommends the following stages:

End of the Project scenario.

Additional Information:

The Chief Executive Officer (CEO) founded the company five years ago. Under her leadership, ABC Company has grown quickly into a successful training company. It delivers a range of accredited professional training.

The Finance Director is also a founder member of ABC Company and is responsible for authorizing budgets for the Operations and Development Teams. She
authorizes all large contracts personally.

The Purchasing Manager reports to the Finance Director and is responsible for managing and monitoring supplier contracts.

The Operations Director is responsible for the delivery off all training and for the training development budget. His department organizes courses, venues and trainers. They work with the Product and the Sales teams to provide a comprehensive training schedule. ABC Company's IT manager reports to the Operations Director.

The Business Development Director has recently been appointed to identify new training needs and propose new products. She will work with the Operations. Director to ensure a cost-conscious approach and that appropriate development technologies are used for the health and safety course.

The Training Development Manager reports to the Business Development Director and is responsible for developing training materials and gaining accreditation, in accordance with the standard course development model. Course developers in his team have skills in a range of development technologies and are allocated to projects as needed.

The Training Delivery Manager, who reports to the Operations Director, is responsible for ensuring that internal and external trainers deliver ABC Company training courses to the required standard. He also checks course materials to ensure they are fit for purpose and of the required quality.

The Central Services Director has responsibility for corporate communications, facilities management and configuration management. He recently led a project to consolidate all company quality systems into one quality management system and set up a corporate quality department, now managed by the Corporate Quality Manager.

The Corporate Document Manager reports to the Central Services Director. She helped establish the company's document management system and now operates it across the business. She manages a team of administrators and contracts staff when workload is high.

The Sales Director joined ABC Company two months ago and is keen to establish himself by suggesting new markets for the courses and material. All account managers and the marketing team report to him. They promote existing training courses to other training companies and existing customers.

End of the additional information.

The delivery of the pilot courses has been split into two separate products: 'planned pilot courses' and 'delivered pilot courses'. 'Planned pilot courses' will be produced during stage 3, and the 'delivered pilot courses' will take place during stage 4. This will allow the project board to approve the plan for the pilot courses before the resources are committed to delivering the pilot courses.
Why is this an appropriate application of the plans theme to control the project?

A. Because a PRINCE2 project should focus on the quality of the products being delivered.
B. Because the pilot courses have been broken down into two separate products.
C. Because the project board should ensure that lessons from one stage are applied to the next stage.
D. Because the delivery steps to create the pilot courses have been aligned to the management stages.

Section: Plans Theme

QUESTION 72
Which of the following statements is False regarding the Risk Management Strategy?

A. It captures and maintains all relevant information on identified threats and opportunities
B. It documents the risk tolerances
C. It documents the approach to risk
D. It identifies responsibilities towards risk for the project

Section: Risk Theme

QUESTION 73
There are four steps in the Risk Management procedure, what are they?

A. Identify, Assess, Resource, Implement
B. Identify, Evaluate, Resource, Implement
C. Identify, Assess, Plan, Implement
D. Identify, Evaluate, Plan, Implement

Section: Risk Theme

QUESTION 74
Which of the following reports does not contain any information on risk?

A. Issue Report
B. Highlight report
C. Lessons Report
D. End Stage Report

Section: Risk Theme

QUESTION 75
Which of the following statements best describes what a risk owner is?

A. Best placed to keep an eye on the risk
B. Carry out the response actions to a risk
C. Responsible for management, monitoring and control of all aspects of a risk
D. Reports to the project manager regularly on the status of a risk

Section: Risk Theme

QUESTION 76
Who is responsible for reviewing the risk management practices to ensure they are in line with the project's risk management strategy?

A. Project Support
B. Project Manager
C. Team Manager
D. Project Assurance

Section: Risk Theme

QUESTION 77
Scenario

A photographer from Portraits Ltd, a professional photographic company, has taken on the role of Team Manager after taking some time to understand the requirements of the project. A contract for their services has been set up and is being monitored by the Purchasing Manager and a Work Package has been agreed. This contract specifies that the photographer must arrange a meeting with the Engineering Manager to establish a schedule for the photo sessions to minimize the impact on the Engineering staff. This meeting should have occurred by now.

The Engineering Manager was made aware of this requirement but when asked he reported that he has received no communication from the photographer. The Project Manager has tried to call the photographer and has had no response. The Project Manager believes there is a risk that Portraits Ltd are overbooking work and prioritizing other clients' work. If Portraits ltd do not deliver on schedule the project will be delayed and the expected benefits will be reduced.

The contract is to be reviewed and Portraits Ltd reminded of their agreement.

The project is now in stage 2. The Project Manager has heard about the possibility of a competitor also producing a calendar to be delivered earlier than the target date for this project. There is a threat that the early release of a competitor's calendar may weaken the impact of the MNO Manufacturing Company calendar, thereby reducing the anticipated benefits of the Calendar project.

Which 2 statements should be recorded under the Risk management procedure heading?

A. When a new problem arises, a full impact analysis will be undertaken to assess the impact on the project' objectives and Business Case.
B. Probability will be assessed against the scales defined in this Risk Management Strategy.
C. Any risk which has an expected value of more than £1 k will NOT be registered.
D. Every threat and opportunity identified must be clearly defined in terms of cause, event and effect.
E. 'Reduce' Response actions which result in a lower impact and/or probability rating.

Section: Risk Theme

QUESTION 78
Scenario

A photographer from Portraits Ltd, a professional photographic company, has taken on the role of Team Manager after taking some time to understand the requirements of the project. A contract for their services has been set up and is being monitored by the Purchasing Manager and a Work Package has been

agreed. This contract specifies that the photographer must arrange a meeting with the Engineering Manager to establish a schedule for the photo sessions to minimize the impact on the Engineering staff. This meeting should have occurred by now.

The Engineering Manager was made aware of this requirement but when asked he reported that he has received no communication from the photographer. The Project Manager has tried to call the photographer and has had no response. The Project Manager believes there is a risk that Portraits Ltd are overbooking work and prioritizing other clients' work. If Portraits ltd do not deliver on schedule the project will be delayed and the expected benefits will be reduced.
The contract is to be reviewed and Portraits Ltd reminded of their agreement.

The project is now in stage 2. The Project Manager has heard about the possibility of a competitor also producing a calendar to be delivered earlier than the target date for this project. There is a threat that the early release of a competitor's calendar may weaken the impact of the MNO Manufacturing Company calendar, thereby reducing the anticipated benefits of the Calendar project.

Which 2 statements should be recorded under either the Records or Reporting headings?

A. Project Support will maintain the Risk Register.
B. The evaluated net effect of all risks will be updated at the end of each stage and included in the End Stage Report.
C. The Change Authority will report monthly to the Project Manager on the status of the change budget.
D. Risks that are likely to occur within the next two weeks should be recorded as imminent.
E. A summary of risks will be maintained and included with the monthly Highlight Reports to the Project Board.

Section: Risk Theme

QUESTION 79
Scenario

A photographer from Portraits Ltd, a professional photographic company, has taken on the role of Team Manager after taking some time to understand the requirements of the project. A contract for their services has been set up and is being monitored by the Purchasing Manager and a Work Package has been agreed. This contract specifies that the photographer must arrange a meeting with the Engineering Manager to establish a schedule for the photo sessions to minimize the impact on the Engineering staff. This meeting should have occurred by now.

The Engineering Manager was made aware of this requirement but when asked he reported that he has received no communication from the photographer. The Project Manager has tried to call the photographer and has had no response. The Project Manager believes there is a risk that Portraits Ltd are overbooking work and prioritizing other clients' work. If Portraits ltd do not deliver on schedule the project will be delayed and the expected benefits will be reduced.
The contract is to be reviewed and Portraits Ltd reminded of their agreement.

The project is now in stage 2. The Project Manager has heard about the possibility of a competitor also producing a calendar to be delivered earlier than the target date for this project. There is a threat that the early release of a competitor's calendar may weaken the impact of the MNO Manufacturing Company calendar, thereby reducing the anticipated benefits of the Calendar project.

Which 2 statements should be recorded under the Timing of risk management activities heading?

A. During stage 4, the selected service provider will manage any risks to their Business Case and report these to the Project Manager on a weekly basis.
B. The Project Board should hold monthly meetings to review project progress.
C. When closing a project, the follow-on action recommendations should be updated with any risks relating to the realization of benefits after the outsourced services go live.
D. Any new risks identified during product development should be reported to the Project Manager by the Team Manager when delivering the completed Work Package.
E. When authorizing a stage, the Project Board will check that the exposure to risk is still acceptable.

Section: Risk Theme

QUESTION 80
Scenario

A photographer from Portraits Ltd, a professional photographic company, has taken on the role of Team Manager after taking some time to understand the requirements of the project. A contract for their services has been set up and is being monitored by the Purchasing Manager and a Work Package has been agreed. This contract specifies that the photographer must arrange a meeting with the Engineering Manager to establish a schedule for the photo sessions to minimize the impact on the Engineering staff. This meeting should have occurred by now.

The Engineering Manager was made aware of this requirement but when asked he reported that he has received no communication from the photographer. The Project Manager has tried to call the photographer and has had no response. The Project Manager believes there is a risk that Portraits Ltd are overbooking work and prioritizing other clients' work. If Portraits ltd do not deliver on schedule the project will be delayed and the expected benefits will be reduced.
The contract is to be reviewed and Portraits Ltd reminded of their agreement.

The project is now in stage 2. The Project Manager has heard about the possibility of a competitor also producing a calendar to be delivered earlier than the target date for this project. There is a threat that the early release of a competitor's calendar may weaken the impact of the MNO Manufacturing Company calendar, thereby reducing the anticipated benefits of the Calendar project.

Which 2 statements should be recorded under the Roles and responsibilities heading?

A. Each risk will be assigned a risk owner.
B. Risks exceeding the agreed project risk tolerance will be reported to the Project Board.
C. Risk tolerances are allocated to each stage by the Project Manager.
D. Project Assurance will ensure that project risks are identified, assessed and controlled according to the agreed risk management procedure.
E. An external consultant is to facilitate a risk identification workshop.

Section: Risk Theme

QUESTION 81
Scenario

A photographer from Portraits Ltd, a professional photographic company, has taken on the role of Team Manager after taking some time to understand the requirements of the project. A contract for their services has been set up and is being monitored by the Purchasing Manager and a Work Package has been agreed. This contract specifies that the photographer must arrange a meeting with the Engineering Manager to establish a schedule for the photo sessions to minimize the impact on the Engineering staff. This meeting should have occurred by now.

The Engineering Manager was made aware of this requirement but when asked he reported that he has received no communication from the photographer. The Project Manager has tried to call the photographer and has had no response. The Project Manager believes there is a risk that Portraits Ltd are overbooking work and prioritizing other clients' work. If Portraits ltd do not deliver on schedule the project will be delayed and the expected benefits will be reduced.
The contract is to be reviewed and Portraits Ltd reminded of their agreement.

The project is now in stage 2. The Project Manager has heard about the possibility of a competitor also producing a calendar to be delivered earlier than the target date for this project. There is a threat that the early release of a competitor's calendar may weaken the impact of the MNO Manufacturing Company calendar, thereby reducing the anticipated benefits of the Calendar project.

Which 2 statements should be recorded under the Proximity heading?

A. Proximity categories for this project are: Imminent; Within the stage; Within the project; Beyond the project.
B. The risk of MFH having no outsourcing experience will be categorized as Stage 4 proximity.
C. Imminent risks are those which may occur within two weeks.
D. Any risk with a proximity category of imminent will be estimated as having a very high impact.
E. The risk of staff leaving the organization will be categorized as beyond the project proximity.

Section: Risk Theme

QUESTION 82
Project Scenario – Health and Safety Training Project:

ABC Company is a well-established training company that uses a standard model to develop training materials and deliver courses to customers.

ABC Company has commissioned a project in response to recent changes in government legislation relating to health and safety on construction sites. The project will deliver "capability to provide health and safety training", including the materials needed for classroom-based training and e-learning. The expected benefits for construction companies include a reduction in lost days and legal costs due to accidents.

The e-learning course will be developed by a specialist external consultancy. The materials for classroom-based training will be delivered by ABC Company's development team. All course materials will be piloted before they are used. ABC Company will deliver training to its customers and also hopes to sell the course materials to other training companies as part of their operational business. ABC Company will use their own sales and marketing departments to promote the courses.

The legislation requires construction companies to comply with the new legislation within two years. The course materials and trainers have to be accredited by a government agency before courses can be delivered. ABC Company is planning to deliver pilot courses within five months of starting the project.

The ABC Company standard development model for new courses recommends the following stages:

End of the Project scenario.

Additional Information:

The <u>Chief Executive Officer (CEO)</u> founded the company five years ago. Under her leadership, ABC Company has grown quickly into a successful training company. It delivers a range of accredited professional training.

The <u>Finance Director</u> is also a founder member of ABC Company and is responsible for authorizing budgets for the Operations and Development Teams. She authorizes all large contracts personally.

The <u>Purchasing Manager</u> reports to the Finance Director and is responsible for managing and monitoring supplier contracts.

The <u>Operations Director</u> is responsible for the delivery off all training and for the training development budget. His department organizes courses, venues and trainers. They work with the Product and the Sales teams to provide a comprehensive training schedule. ABC Company's IT manager reports to the Operations Director.

The <u>Business Development</u> Director has recently been appointed to identify new training needs and propose new products. She will work with the Operations. Director to ensure a cost-conscious approach and that appropriate development technologies are used for the health and safety course.

The <u>Training Development Manager</u> reports to the Business Development Director and is responsible for developing training materials and gaining accreditation, in accordance with the standard course development model. Course developers in his team have skills in a range of development technologies and are allocated to projects as needed.

The <u>Training Delivery Manager</u>, who reports to the Operations Director, is responsible for ensuring that internal and external trainers deliver ABC Company training courses to the required standard. He also checks course materials to ensure they are fit for purpose and of the required quality.

The <u>Central Services Director</u> has responsibility for corporate communications, facilities management and configuration management. He recently led a project to consolidate all company quality systems into one quality management system and set up a corporate quality department, now managed by the Corporate Quality Manager.

The <u>Corporate Document Manager</u> reports to the Central Services Director. She

helped establish the company's document management system and now operates it across the business. She manages a team of administrators and contracts staff when workload is high.

The Sales Director joined ABC Company two months ago and is keen to establish himself by suggesting new markets for the courses and material. All account managers and the marketing team report to him. They promote existing training courses to other training companies and existing customers.

End of the additional information.

ABC Company carried out a similar project two years ago, in response to changes in health and safety legislation for the health service. The experiences from that project were used to refine the corporate risk management policy. For that reason, the project board decided to use the corporate risk management policy in the risk management approach for this project.
Is this appropriate, and why?

A. Yes, because experience from previous projects should be taken into account in the risk management approach.
B. Yes, because the corporate risk management policy was updated, as a result of lessons from previous projects.
C. No, because the risk management approach should be tailored to suit the project and its environment.
D. No, because a separate risk management approach is not necessary when the company has a risk management policy.

Section: Risk Theme

QUESTION 83
Which of the following is the definition for an off-specification?

A. An issue the Project Manager needs to resolve or escalate
B. Something forecast or currently not meeting specification
C. A proposal for a change to a baseline
D. A statement of concern

Section: Change Theme

QUESTION 84
In which strategy would the change control process be recorded?

A. Quality Management Strategy
B. Configuration Management Strategy
C. Risk Management Strategy
D. Communication Management Strategy

Section: Change Theme

QUESTION 85
If the Project Board are too busy to authorize all change requests themselves they can appoint?

A. A Change Authority
B. A Change Board
C. A Change Committee
D. A Change Budget

Section: Change Theme

QUESTION 86
What is the purpose of a Product Status Account?

A. A set of records that describe information about the project
B. A log used to record problems or concerns about products
C. An audit or review to compare actual status of products
D. A report covering the status about the state of the projects products within

Section: Change Theme

QUESTION 87
When examining a project issue, which three aspects should be considered?
1. Performance targets
2. Business Case
3. Resources
4. Risk

A. 1, 3, 4
B. 2, 3, 4
C. 1, 2, 4
D. 1, 2, 3

Section: Change Theme

QUESTION 88
Who would be responsible for maintaining the Configuration Item Records?

A. Project Manager
B. Project Support
C. Project Assurance
D. Team Manager

Section: Change Theme

QUESTION 89
HOTSPOT

Scenario

A photographer from Portraits Ltd, a professional photographic company, has taken on the role of Team Manager after taking some time to understand the requirements of the project. A contract for their services has been set up and is being monitored by the Purchasing Manager and a Work Package has been agreed. This contract specifies that the photographer must arrange a meeting with the Engineering Manager to establish a schedule for the photo sessions to minimize the impact on the Engineering staff. This meeting should have occurred by now.

The Engineering Manager was made aware of this requirement but when asked he reported that he has received no communication from the photographer. The Project Manager has tried to call the photographer and has had no response. The Project Manager believes there is a risk that Portraits Ltd are overbooking work and prioritizing other clients' work. If Portraits ltd do not deliver on schedule the project will be delayed and the expected benefits will be reduced.
The contract is to be reviewed and Portraits Ltd reminded of their agreement.

The project is now in stage 2. The Project Manager has heard about the possibility of a competitor also producing a calendar to be delivered earlier than the target date for this project. There is a threat that the early release of a competitor's calendar may weaken the impact of the MNO Manufacturing Company calendar, thereby reducing the anticipated benefits of the Calendar project.

There is a major concern over an apparent lack of control of project documentation.

For each concern listed in Column 1, select from Column 2 the configuration management task that could help address the problem. Each selection from Column 2 can be used once, more than once or not at all.

Hot Area:

Section: Change Theme

QUESTION 90
Scenario:

The Ministry of Food Hygiene (MFH) has a quality management system which contains a document control process to manage all documentation requirements. The document control process was created by the MFH Quality Manager, who now maintains all of MFH's documents and performs an organization-wide configuration management role. The MFH Quality Manager will administer the configuration management procedure for the Restructuring project since this must comply with the MFH document control process.

According to PRINCE2, which statement about the Configuration Management Strategy for the Outsourcing project is correct?

A. Every project needs a Configuration Management Strategy, even if the organization has existing configuration management standards, because every project has different circumstances.
B. A separate Configuration Management Strategy will be required for each of the suppliers within this project because each will have a different way of managing and storing products.
C. A Configuration Management Strategy is unnecessary for this project because the MFH document control process is documented. It is acceptable simply to reference this in the Quality Management Strategy.

Section: Change Theme

QUESTION 91
Scenario:

The Ministry of Food Hygiene (MFH) has a quality management system which contains a document control process to manage all documentation requirements. The document control process was created by the MFH Quality Manager, who now maintains all of MFH's documents and performs an organization-wide configuration management role. The MFH Quality Manager will administer the configuration management procedure for the Restructuring project since this must comply with the MFH document control process.

According to PRINCE2, which statement about appointing the MFH Quality Manager to administer the configuration management procedure is correct?

A. The MFH Quality Manager should administer the configuration management procedure on this project because this task should always be assigned to corporate or programme management.
B. The MFH Quality Manager should only administer the configuration management procedure on one project at a time. If the MFH Quality Manager already performs this task on another project, another individual should be appointed.
C. The MFH Quality Manager would be suitable to perform this task because he is the author of the document control process and is likely to have the knowledge required for this role.

Section: Change Theme

QUESTION 92
Scenario:

The Ministry of Food Hygiene (MFH) has a quality management system which contains a document control process to manage all documentation requirements. The document control process was created by the MFH Quality Manager, who now maintains all of MFH's documents and performs an organization-wide configuration management role. The MFH Quality Manager will administer the configuration management procedure for the Restructuring project since this must comply with the MFH document control process.

What products will be impacted by this change?

A. All of the project's products created so far.
B. Only those products created in the first three weeks of stage 3.
C. All of the project's products which relate to or include services provided by the Facilities Division.
D. No products would need to be changed but some will need to be removed from the project.

Section: Change Theme

QUESTION 93
Scenario:

The Ministry of Food Hygiene (MFH) has a quality management system which contains a document control process to manage all documentation requirements. The document control process was created by the MFH Quality Manager, who now maintains all of MFH's documents and performs an organization-wide configuration management role. The MFH Quality Manager will administer the configuration management procedure for the Restructuring project since this must comply with the MFH document control process.
What additional risk will this place on the project?

A. None because risks associated with the centralization and rationalization of the Facilities Division will be managed by another project.
B. These changes will delay stage 3 by three weeks.
C. There is only £70k left in the project change budget.
D. The reduced value of the contracted services required by the Outsourcing project may result in an insufficient number of proposals being received.

Section: Change Theme

QUESTION 94
Scenario:

The Ministry of Food Hygiene (MFH) has a quality management system which contains a document control process to manage all documentation requirements. The document control process was created by the MFH Quality Manager, who now maintains all of MFH's documents and performs an organization-wide configuration management role. The MFH Quality Manager will administer the configuration management procedure for the Restructuring project since this must comply with the MFH document control process.
What will be the impact on the benefits?

A. Reduced savings, now £10m over 10 years.
B. Increased savings of £5m over 10 years from the new initiative to centralize the services provided by the Facilities Division.
C. An additional cost of £1.5m to deliver the services provided by the Facilities Division.
D. Outsourcing project cost reduced by 50%.

Section: Change Theme

QUESTION 95
If Project tolerances were threatened, who needs to be notified?

A. Project Board
B. Project Manager
C. Corporate or Programme Management
D. Executive

Section: Progress Theme

QUESTION 96
During which process would the stage tolerances be set?

A. Controlling a Stage
B. Initiating a Project
C. Managing a Stage Boundary
D. Directing a Project

Section: Progress Theme

QUESTION 97
Which of the following is not a factor to consider when determining the length of a stage?

A. The amount of resources available h the short term
B. How far ahead you can sensibly plan n detail
C. The technical stages within the project
D. The amount of risk associated with the project

Section: Progress Theme

QUESTION 98
There are two time driven controls in PRINCE2, which are they?

A. Highlight and End Stage Reports
B. Highlight and Checkpoint Reports
C. Checkpoint and End Project Reports
D. Highlight and Lessons Reports

Section: Progress Theme

QUESTION 99

Who is responsible for confirming stage and project progress against agreed tolerances?

A. Project Support
B. Executive
C. Project Assurance
D. Project Manager

Section: Progress Theme

QUESTION 100
Project Scenario

Calendar Project (Note: The companies and people within the scenario are fictional.)

There has been a reduction in fie number of orders at the MNO Manufacturing Company due in part to the increased marketing activities of its competitors. To help counter this, the company has decided to create a promotional calendar for next year for all its current and prospective customers. The end product of this project will be a prepared calendar pack, ready for printing. The design of the calendar will be similar to one sent out previously, and must reflect the company image as described in the existing corporate branding standards. Another project is currently producing a new company logo when is to be printed on each page of the promotional calendar. The prepared calendar pack will consist of:
- Design for each month - correctly showing at public holidays and new company logo
- Selected photographs- 12 professionally-produced photographs, showing
- different members of staff Selected paper and selected envelope - for printing and mailing the calendar
- Chosen label design - a competition to design a label will be held as part of
- this project List of customers - names and addresses of customers to whom the calendar will be sent.

The project is currently in initiation and will have two further stages:

Stage 2 will include tie activities to:
- Create the customer fast using information from the Accounts and
- Marketing departments Confirm compliance with the Data Protection Legislation
- Create a design for each month - this will be done by the internal creative
- team Select and appoint a professional photographer
- Gather photograph design ideas from previous project and agree

photographic session schedule Prepare a production cost forecast
- Select paper and envelope.

Stage 3 will include the activities to:
- Produce and select tie professionally-taken photographs
- Hold the label design competition and choose the label design
- Assemble the prepared calendar pack.

A production cost forecast, based on the options and costs for the paper, envelope, printing and marketing of the calendar is to be produced in stage 2. However, the actual production and distribution of the calendars is not within the scope of the project. The product cost forecast will be reviewed by the Project Board to

determine whether tie project should continue.

It is now 05 October and the prepared calendar pack must be delivered to the print company by 30 November, to enable printing and distribution of the calendar in time for Christmas. The cost of the activities to develop the specialist products and the cost of the project management activities are estimated to be £20,000. There is a project time tolerance of +1 week /-2 weeks and a project cost tolerance of +£6,000 / -£6,000. A change budget of £500 has been allocated but there is no risk budget.

During stage 2, if the Project Manager decides to recommend that the Project Plan is revised to finish three weeks later, which statement is correct?

A. The tolerances stated in the Project Plan CANNOT be changed.
B. The Executive needs to seek formal approval from corporate management to implement this change.
C. The current project must close prematurely and be restarted with a new Project Plan, a new Business Case and new Risk Register.
D. The revision of the Project Plan would have to wait until the end stage assessment of stage 2.

Section: Progress Theme

QUESTION 101
Project Scenario

Calendar Project (Note: The companies and people within the scenario are fictional.)

There has been a reduction in fie number of orders at the MNO Manufacturing Company due in part to the increased marketing activities of its competitors. To help counter this, the company has decided to create a promotional calendar for next year for all its current and prospective customers. The end product of this project will be a prepared calendar pack, ready for printing. The design of the calendar will be similar to one sent out previously, and must reflect the company image as described in the existing corporate branding standards. Another project is currently producing a new company logo when is to be printed on each page of the promotional calendar. The prepared calendar pack will consist of:
- Design for each month - correctly showing at public holidays and new company logo
- Selected photographs- 12 professionally-produced photographs, showing
- different members of staff Selected paper and selected envelope - for printing and mailing the calendar
- Chosen label design - a competition to design a label will be held as part of
- this project List of customers - names and addresses of customers to whom the calendar will be sent

The project is currently in initiation and will have two further stages: Stage 2 will include tie activities to:
- Create the customer fast using information from the Accounts and Marketing departments
- Confirm compliance with the Data Protection Legislation
- Create a design for each month - this will be done by the internal creative
- team Select and appoint a professional photographer
- Gather photograph design ideas from previous project and agree
- photographic session schedule Prepare a production cost forecast
- Select paper and envelope.

Stage 3 will include the activities to:
- Produce and select tie professionally-taken photographs
- Hold the label design competition and choose the label design Assemble
- the prepared calendar pack.

A production cost forecast, based on the options and costs for the paper, envelope, printing and marketing of the calendar is to be produced in stage 2. However, the actual production and distribution of the calendars is not within the scope of the project. The product cost forecast will be reviewed by the Project Board to determine whether tie project should continue.

It is now 05 October and the prepared calendar pack must be delivered to the print company by 30 November, to enable printing and distribution of the calendar in time for Christmas. The cost of the activities to develop the specialist products and the cost of the project management activities are estimated to be £20,000. There is a project time tolerance of +1 week /-2 weeks and a project cost tolerance of +£6,000 / -£6,000. A change budget of £500 has been allocated but there is no risk budget.

As the project approaches the end of stage 2, the Project Manager has requested a Product Status Account to ensure that all products are at their expected point of development. Although the list of customers has been quality reviewed, it has not been baselined because the Marketing department have not provided all of the prospective customers' details. What initial action should the Project Manager take?

A. Delay producing the End Stage Report until the list of customers has been baselined.
B. Raise an Exception Report to the Project Board to highlight the issue.
C. Check the target sign-off date for the list of customers.
D. Update the product status to baselined and obtain a commitment from the Marketing department to finish this work within the next few days.

Section: Progress Theme

QUESTION 102
Project Scenario

Calendar Project (Note: The companies and people within the scenario are fictional.)

There has been a reduction in fie number of orders at the MNO Manufacturing Company due in part to the increased marketing activities of its competitors. To help counter this, the company has decided to create a promotional calendar for next year for all its current and prospective customers. The end product of this project will be a prepared calendar pack, ready for printing. The design of the calendar will be similar to one sent out previously, and must reflect the company image as described in the existing corporate branding standards. Another project is currently producing a new company logo when is to be printed on each page of the promotional calendar. The prepared calendar pack will consist of:
- Design for each month - correctly showing at public holidays and new company logo
- Selected photographs- 12 professionally-produced photographs, showing
- different members of staff Selected paper and selected envelope - for printing and mailing the calendar

- Chosen label design - a competition to design a label will be held as part of this project List of customers - names and addresses of customers to whom the calendar will be sent.

The project is currently in initiation and will have two further stages:

Stage 2 will include tie activities to:
- Create the customer fast using information from the Accounts and
- Marketing departments Confirm compliance with the Data Protection Legislation
- Create a design for each month - this will be done by the internal creative
- team Select and appoint a professional photographer
- Gather photograph design ideas from previous project and agree
- photographic session schedule Prepare a production cost forecast
- Select paper and envelope.

Stage 3 will include the activities to:
- Produce and select tie professionally-taken photographs
- Hold the label design competition and choose the label design Assemble
- the prepared calendar pack.

A production cost forecast, based on the options and costs for the paper, envelope, printing and marketing of the calendar is to be produced in stage 2. However, the actual production and distribution of the calendars is not within the scope of the project. The product cost forecast will be reviewed by the Project Board to determine whether tie project should continue.

It is now 05 October and the prepared calendar pack must be delivered to the print company by 30 November, to enable printing and distribution of the calendar in time for Christmas. The cost of the activities to develop the specialist products and the cost of the project management activities are estimated to be £20,000. There is a project time tolerance of +1 week /-2 weeks and a project cost tolerance of +£6,000 / -£6,000. A change budget of £500 has been allocated but there is no risk budget.

The team member collating the list of customers has now forecast that it will NOT be complete by the end of this stage as originally planned, due to a number of new prospective customers' details not yet being available. What action should the team member take?

A. Report the forecast delay in the next Checkpoint Report to the Executive.
B. Add the product to the next Stage Plan in order to allocate additional resources and complete the work.
C. Make an entry in the Risk Register so the Project Manager can decide on appropriate action.
D. Raise an issue to inform the Project Manager.

QUESTION 103
Scenario:

Techniques, processes and procedures
1. Any threat that may result in a loss of MFH data must be escalated immediately.

Joint agreements
2. Work is to start at the beginning of week 2 (Stage 4).
3. The project will take two years to complete, at an estimated cost of £2.5m.

Tolerances
4. None.

Constraints
5. MFH staff must not be involved in any heavy lifting during the removal of existing IT equipment.
6. Installation work must take place during MFH normal working hours. 7. +£10,000 / -£25,000.

Reporting arrangements
8. Highlight Report every Monday by 10.00 am.
9. The report must contain a summary of all products worked on during the previous week.
10. Project Manager must be notified of any issues immediately by telephone.

Problem handling and escalation
11. Impact analysis of all issues must be completed within 24 hours.

Extracts or references
12. The Stage Plan for stage 4 is available from Project Support.

Approval method
13. Project Assurance will review the completed Work Package and confirm completion

Which 2 statements apply to either the Techniques, processes and procedures or Constraints sections?

A. Delete entry 1 because this section should contain the techniques, processes and procedures required for specialist product development.
B. Add 'There must be minimum disruption to current services' to Constraints.
C. Move entry 5 to Techniques, processes and procedures because this is a technique which staff should be aware of.
D. Delete entry 6 because this applies to Office Moves Limited and is therefore outside the Work Package.
E. Delete entry 7 because this should be contained in the Quality skills required section of the Product Description.

Section: Progress Theme

QUESTION 104
Scenario:

Techniques, processes and procedures
1. Any threat that may result in a loss of MFH data must be escalated immediately.

Joint agreements
2. Work is to start at the beginning of week 2 (Stage 4).
3. The project will take two years to complete, at an estimated cost of £2.5m.

Tolerances
4. None.

Constraints
5. MFH staff must not be involved in any heavy lifting during the removal of existing IT equipment.
6. Installation work must take place during MFH normal working hours.
7. +£10,000 / -£25,000.

Reporting arrangements
8. Highlight Report every Monday by 10.00 am.
9. The report must contain a summary of all products worked on during the previous week.
10. Project Manager must be notified of any issues immediately by telephone.

Problem handling and escalation
11. Impact analysis of all issues must be completed within 24 hours.

Extracts or references
12. The Stage Plan for stage 4 is available from Project Support.

Approval method
13. Project Assurance will review the completed Work Package and confirm completion

Which 2 statements apply to either the Reporting arrangements or Problem handling and escalation sections?

A. Replace entry 8 with 'Checkpoint Report every Monday by 10.00 am' because Highlight Reports are intended for the Project Board.

B. Delete entry 9 because this level of detail is unnecessary.

C. Move entry 10 to Problem handling and escalation because that section describes how issues are handled.

D. Add 'Any risks identified to be added to the Risk Register' to Reporting arrangements.

E. Delete entry 11 because the impact analysis should be provided when the issue is notified.

Section: Progress Theme

QUESTION 105
Scenario:

Techniques, processes and procedures
1. Any threat that may result in a loss of MFH data must be escalated immediately.

Joint agreements
2. Work is to start at the beginning of week 2 (Stage 4).
3. The project will take two years to complete, at an estimated cost of £2.5m.

Tolerances
4. None.

Constraints
5. MFH staff must not be involved in any heavy lifting during the removal of existing IT equipment.
6. Installation work must take place during MFH normal working hours. 7.
+£10,000 / -£25,000.

Reporting arrangements
8. Highlight Report every Monday by 10.00 am.
9. The report must contain a summary of all products worked on during the previous week.
10. Project Manager must be notified of any issues immediately by telephone.

Problem handling and escalation
11. Impact analysis of all issues must be completed within 24 hours.

Extracts or references
12. The Stage Plan for stage 4 is available from Project Support.

Approval method
13. Project Assurance will review the completed Work Package and confirm completion

Which 2 statements apply to either the Extracts or references or Approval method sections?

A. Delete entry 12 because this should be the Team Plan not the Stage Plan.

B. A suitable entry for Extracts or references would be 'Product Descriptions are available from Project Support'.

C. Move entry 13 to Reporting arrangements because this describes how completion will be advised to the

D. Project Manager.

E. Delete entry 13 because this is NOT a Project Assurance responsibility.

F. Add 'The Project Manager is to be advised of completion of the Work Package by email'.

Section: Progress Theme

QUESTION 106
DRAG DROP

Project Scenario – Health and Safety Training Project:

ABC Company is a well-established training company that uses a standard model to develop training materials and deliver courses to customers.

ABC Company has commissioned a project in response to recent changes in government legislation relating to health and safety on construction sites. The project will deliver "capability to provide health and safety training", including the materials needed for classroom-based training and e-learning. The expected benefits for construction companies include a reduction in lost days and legal costs due to accidents.

The e-learning course will be developed by a specialist external consultancy. The materials for classroom-based training will be delivered by ABC Company's development team. All course materials will be piloted before they are used. ABC Company will deliver training to its customers and also hopes to sell the course materials to other training companies as part of their operational business. ABC Company will use their own sales and marketing departments to promote the courses.

The legislation requires construction companies to comply with the new legislation within two years. The course materials and trainers have to be accredited by a government agency before courses can be delivered. ABC Company is planning to deliver pilot courses within five months of starting the project.

The ABC Company standard development model for new courses recommends the following stages:

End of the Project scenario.

Additional Information:

The Chief Executive Officer (CEO) founded the company five years ago. Under her leadership, ABC Company has grown quickly into a successful training company. It delivers a range of accredited professional training.

The Finance Director is also a founder member of ABC Company and is responsible for authorizing budgets for the Operations and Development Teams. She authorizes all large contracts personally.

The Purchasing Manager reports to the Finance Director and is responsible for managing and monitoring supplier contracts.

The Operations Director is responsible for the delivery off all training and for the training development budget. His department organizes courses, venues and trainers. They work with the Product and the Sales teams to provide a comprehensive training schedule. ABC Company's IT manager reports to the Operations Director.

The Business Development Director has recently been appointed to identify new training needs and propose new products. She will work with the Operations. Director to ensure a cost-conscious approach and that appropriate development technologies are used for the health and safety course.

The Training Development Manager reports to the Business Development Director and is responsible for developing training materials and gaining accreditation, in accordance with the standard course development model. Course developers in his team have skills in a range of development technologies and are allocated to projects as needed.

The Training Delivery Manager, who reports to the Operations Director, is responsible for ensuring that internal and external trainers deliver ABC Company training courses to the required standard. He also checks course materials to ensure they are fit for purpose and of the required quality.

The Central Services Director has responsibility for corporate communications, facilities management and configuration management. He recently led a project to consolidate all company quality systems into one quality management system and set up a corporate quality department, now managed by the Corporate Quality Manager.

The Corporate Document Manager reports to the Central Services Director. She helped establish the company's document management system and now operates it across the business. She manages a team of administrators and contracts staff when workload is high.

The Sales Director joined ABC Company two months ago and is keen to establish himself by suggesting new markets for the courses and material. All account managers and the marketing team report to him. They promote existing training courses to other training companies and existing customers.

End of the additional information. PROGRESS

Here are three statements related to tolerances for the Health and Safety Training Project. For each statement, select the tolerance area (A-E) it represents. Choose only one tolerance area for each statement. Each tolerance area can be used once, more than once, or not at all.

Select and Place:

The 'e-learning course' will be accessible by users for 10 hrs each day +/- 2 hrs per day.	Time
The 'classroom-based training material' must include slides and exercises. It should also include pre-course reading.	Cost
Company A plans to generate £1000,000 +/- 10%.	Scope
	Quality
	Benefits

Section: Progress Theme

QUESTION 107

Project Scenario – Health and Safety Training Project:

ABC Company is a well-established training company that uses a standard model to develop training materials and deliver courses to customers.

ABC Company has commissioned a project in response to recent changes in government legislation relating to health and safety on construction sites. The project will deliver "capability to provide health and safety training", including the materials needed for classroom-based training and e-learning. The expected benefits for construction companies include a reduction in lost days and legal costs due to accidents.

The e-learning course will be developed by a specialist external consultancy. The materials for classroom-based training will be delivered by ABC Company's development team. All course materials will be piloted before they are used. ABC Company will deliver training to its customers and also hopes to sell the course materials to other training companies as part of their operational business. ABC

Company will use their own sales and marketing departments to promote the courses.

The legislation requires construction companies to comply with the new legislation within two years. The course materials and trainers have to be accredited by a government agency before courses can be delivered. ABC Company is planning to deliver pilot courses within five months of starting the project.

The ABC Company standard development model for new courses recommends the following stages:

End of the Project scenario.

Additional Information:

The Chief Executive Officer (CEO) founded the company five years ago. Under her leadership, ABC Company has grown quickly into a successful training company. It delivers a range of accredited professional training.

The Finance Director is also a founder member of ABC Company and is responsible for authorizing budgets for the Operations and Development Teams. She authorizes all large contracts personally.

The Purchasing Manager reports to the Finance Director and is responsible for managing and monitoring supplier contracts.

The Operations Director is responsible for the delivery off all training and for the training development budget. His department organizes courses, venues and trainers. They work with the Product and the Sales teams to provide a comprehensive training schedule. ABC Company's IT manager reports to the Operations Director.

The Business Development Director has recently been appointed to identify new training needs and propose new products. She will work with the Operations. Director to ensure a cost-conscious approach and that appropriate development technologies are used for the health and safety course.

The Training Development Manager reports to the Business Development Director and is responsible for developing training materials and gaining accreditation, in accordance with the standard course development model. Course developers in his team have skills in a range of development technologies and are allocated to projects as needed.

The Training Delivery Manager, who reports to the Operations Director, is responsible for ensuring that internal and external trainers deliver ABC Company training courses to the required standard. He also checks course materials to ensure they are fit for purpose and of the required quality.

The Central Services Director has responsibility for corporate communications, facilities management and configuration management. He recently led a project to consolidate all company quality systems into one quality management system and set up a corporate quality department, now managed by the Corporate Quality Manager.

The Corporate Document Manager reports to the Central Services Director. She helped establish the company's document management system and now operates it across the business. She manages a team of administrators and contracts staff when workload is high.

The Sales Director joined ABC Company two months ago and is keen to establish himself by suggesting new markets for the courses and material. All account managers and the marketing team report to him. They promote existing training courses to other training companies and existing customers.

End of the additional information.

The external team manager for the 'e-learning course' has reviewed the quality register to ensure all quality activities have been completed. The 'e-learning course' has been approved and accreditation has been achieved. As a result, the team manager updated the work package to notify the project manager that it is complete, and updated the team plan.
Is this appropriate, and why?

A. Yes, because the project manager needs to receive confirmation that work has been completed and approved.
B. Yes, because a team plan to gain accreditation of the 'e-learning course' is required to be part of the work package.
C. No, because it is the configuration item record of the relevant product description that is updated, not the work package.
D. No, because the work package should be checked to confirm the reporting arrangements of the 'e-learning course'.

Section: Progress Theme

QUESTION 108
Starting Up a project is triggered by which of the following?

A. Legislation
B. Corporate Strategy

C. Risks
D. Mandate

Section: Starting up and Initiating a Project

QUESTION 109
Who is responsible for appointing the Project Manager?

A. Corporate or Programme Management
B. The Project Board
C. The Executive
D. Project Assurance

Section: Starting up and Initiating a Project

QUESTION 110
During which of the following activities is the Project Product Description created?

A. Design and appoint the Project Management Team
B. Prepare the outline business case
C. Select the project approach and assemble the project brief
D. Plan the initiation stage

Section: Starting up and Initiating a Project

QUESTION 111
Which other management product is created when the Business case is updated during Initiating a Project?

A. Post project review plan
B. Risk Register
C. Benefits Review plan
D. Issue Register

Section: Starting up and Initiating a Project

QUESTION 112
Scenario
Additional Information

Extract from the Communication Management Strategy.

The project information in the table below is true, but it may not be recorded under the correct heading or be in the correct document.

Introduction	1. This document contains details of how the project management team will send information to individuals working on the Calendar project, and receive information from them.
Communication procedure	2. See MNO Manufacturing Company standards for all internal company communications.
Tools and techniques	3. Use the staff newsletter to launch the label design competition and to promote the chosen label design. 4. Using the number of responses to the label design competition as a measure, report fortnightly to the Project Board on the effectiveness of the staff newsletter as a vehicle for communication. 5. Use the company website to advertise the promotional calendar to customers.
Records	6. A record should be maintained for each product of the project. As a minimum this should show the project name, product name, product title, and version number. 7. External email and correspondence relating to the Calendar project should be recorded electronically in the project folder. 8. Information received in hard copy should, where possible, should be scanned and filed as above.
Timing of communication activities	9. At the end of each stage, audit and report on the performance of the communication methods being used. 10. Highlight Reports to be provided to appropriate stakeholders, at the frequency defined in each Stage Plan.
Stakeholder analysis: Interested parties	11. Photographer. 12. Print company.
Information needs for each interested party	13. Weekly updates will be provided by email to the individual producing the staff newsletter. 14. Engineering Manager is to be consulted when preparing the photo session schedule.

Using the Project Scenario, select the appropriate response to each of the following 5 questions which have been raised by the Project Board.

The project is now at the end of the initiation stage. Having decided that the Calendar project is a relatively simple project, the Project Manager combined the Starting Up a Project process and the Initiating a Project process. No Project Brief has been produced. Instead the Project Manager used the project mandate to produce a simple Project Initiation Documentation (PIO). The PIO includes the Business Case, a product checklist and several Product Descriptions, Including the Project Product Description. Short sections are also included for each of the strategies and the controls to be applied. The Project Manager has elected to use the Daily Log to record all risks, issues. lessons and quality - results.

After the initiation stage there will be two further stages during which a small number of Work Packages will be authorized. While these are being managed, the Project Manager will hold regular checkpoints, which will support the production of weekly Highlight Reports to the Project Board.

There is no Project Brief. How can there be a common understanding of the desired outcomes for the prepared calendar pack?

A. The simple Project Initiation Documentation contains the Quality Management Strategy. This contains details of the acceptance criteria for this project.
B. The Project Brief should have been produced and approved before the project progressed into the initiation stage.
C. The simple Project Initiation Documentation contains the project definition.

Section: Starting up and Initiating a Project

QUESTION 113
Scenario
Additional Information

Extract from the Communication Management Strategy.
The project information in the table below is true, but it may not be recorded under the correct heading or be in the correct document.

Introduction	1. This document contains details of how the project management team will send information to individuals working on the Calendar project, and receive information from them.
Communication procedure	2. See MNO Manufacturing Company standards for all internal company communications.
Tools and techniques	3. Use the staff newsletter to launch the label design competition and to promote the chosen label design. 4. Using the number of responses to the label design competition as a measure, report fortnightly to the Project Board on the effectiveness of the staff newsletter as a vehicle for communication. 5. Use the company website to advertise the promotional calendar to customers.
Records	6. A record should be maintained for each product of the project. As a minimum this should show the project name, product name, product title, and version number. 7. External email and correspondence relating to the Calendar project should be recorded electronically in the project folder. 8. Information received in hard copy should, where possible, should be scanned and filed as above.
Timing of communication activities	9. At the end of each stage, audit and report on the performance of the communication methods being used. 10. Highlight Reports to be provided to appropriate stakeholders, at the frequency defined in each Stage Plan.
Stakeholder analysis: Interested parties	11. Photographer. 12. Print company.
Information needs for each interested party	13. Weekly updates will be provided by email to the individual producing the staff newsletter. 14. Engineering Manager is to be consulted when preparing the photo session schedule.

Using the Project Scenario, select the appropriate response to each of the following 5 questions which have been raised by the Project Board.

The project is now at the end of the initiation stage. Having decided that the Calendar project is a relatively simple project, the Project Manager combined the Starting Up a Project process and the Initiating a Project process. No Project Brief has been produced. Instead the Project Manager used the project mandate to produce a simple Project Initiation Documentation (PID). The PID includes the Business Case, a product checklist and several Product Descriptions, including the Project Product Description. Short sections are also included for each of the strategies and the controls to be applied. The Project Manager has elected to use the Daily Log to record all risks, issues, lessons and quality - results.

After the initiation stage there will be two further stages during which a small number of Work Packages will be authorized. While these are being managed, the Project Manager will hold regular checkpoints, which will support the production of weekly Highlight Reports to the Project Board.

There is no mention of any Stage Plans, yet there are two further stages proposed. How will this be resolved?

A. It is appropriate for the Calendar project to be run as two further stages as there is a key decision to be made at the end of stage 2. Stage Plans will be produced.
B. Whilst the activities are divided into two further stages, there is no reason why the Calendar project should use stages. The project will therefore be run as a single stage project and the activities will be added to the Initiation Stage Plan.
C. There will be three Stage Plans, the two management stages plus an additional stage to plan and complete the activities of the Closing a Project process.

Section: Starting up and Initiating a Project

QUESTION 114
Scenario
Additional Information

Extract from the Communication Management Strategy.
The project information in the table below is true, but it may not be recorded under the correct heading or be in the correct document.

Introduction	1. This document contains details of how the project management team will send information to individuals working on the Calendar project, and receive information from them.
Communication procedure	2. See MNO Manufacturing Company standards for all internal company communications.
Tools and techniques	3. Use the staff newsletter to launch the label design competition and to promote the chosen label design. 4. Using the number of responses to the label design competition as a measure, report fortnightly to the Project Board on the effectiveness of the staff newsletter as a vehicle for communication. 5. Use the company website to advertise the promotional calendar to customers.
Records	6. A record should be maintained for each product of the project. As a minimum this should show the project name, product name, product title, and version number. 7. External email and correspondence relating to the Calendar project should be recorded electronically in the project folder. 8. Information received in hard copy should, where possible, should be scanned and filed as above.
Timing of communication activities	9. At the end of each stage, audit and report on the performance of the communication methods being used. 10. Highlight Reports to be provided to appropriate stakeholders, at the frequency defined in each Stage Plan.
Stakeholder analysis: Interested parties	11. Photographer. 12. Print company.
Information needs for each interested party	13. Weekly updates will be provided by email to the individual producing the staff newsletter. 14. Engineering Manager is to be consulted when preparing the photo session schedule.

Using the Project Scenario, select the appropriate response to each of the following 5 questions which have been raised by the Project Board.

The project is now at the end of the initiation stage. Having decided that the Calendar project is a relatively simple project, the Project Manager combined the Starting Up a Project process and the Initiating a Project process. No Project Brief has been produced. Instead the Project Manager used the project mandate to produce a simple Project Initiation Documentation (PIO). The PIO includes the Business Case, a product checklist and several Product Descriptions, Including the Project Product Description. Short sections are also included for each of the strategies and the controls to be applied. The Project Manager has elected to use the Daily Log to record all risks, issues, lessons and quality - results.
After the initiation stage there will be two further stages during which a small number of Work Packages will be authorized. While these are being managed, the Project Manager will hold regular checkpoints, which will support the production of weekly Highlight Reports to the Project Board.

No Benefits Review Plan has been developed. Where should the schedule of benefit reviews be recorded?

A. As deliverables of the project, all benefit reviews should be scheduled and documented in the Project Plan during initiation.
B. Small projects do not require a schedule of benefit reviews as only one review is required towards the end of the project and this should be documented within the Business Case.
C. Benefit reviews should be planned and recorded in the simple PID.

Section: Starting up and Initiating a Project

QUESTION 115
Scenario
Additional Information

Extract from the Communication Management Strategy.
The project information in the table below is true, but it may not be recorded under the correct heading or be in the correct document.

Introduction	1. This document contains details of how the project management team will send information to individuals working on the Calendar project, and receive information from them.
Communication procedure	2. See MNO Manufacturing Company standards for all internal company communications.
Tools and techniques	3. Use the staff newsletter to launch the label design competition and to promote the chosen label design. 4. Using the number of responses to the label design competition as a measure, report fortnightly to the Project Board on the effectiveness of the staff newsletter as a vehicle for communication. 5. Use the company website to advertise the promotional calendar to customers.
Records	6. A record should be maintained for each product of the project. As a minimum this should show the project name, product name, product title, and version number. 7. External email and correspondence relating to the Calendar project should be recorded electronically in the project folder. 8. Information received in hard copy should, where possible, should be scanned and filed as above.
Timing of communication activities	9. At the end of each stage, audit and report on the performance of the communication methods being used. 10. Highlight Reports to be provided to appropriate stakeholders, at the frequency defined in each Stage Plan.
Stakeholder analysis: Interested parties	11. Photographer. 12. Print company.
Information needs for each interested party	13. Weekly updates will be provided by email to the individual producing the staff newsletter. 14. Engineering Manager is to be consulted when preparing the photo session schedule.

Using the Project Scenario, select the appropriate response to each of the following 5 questions which have been raised by the Project Board.

The project is now at the end of the initiation stage. Having decided that the Calendar project is a relatively simple project, the Project Manager combined the Starting Up a Project process and the Initiating a Project process. No Project Brief has been produced. Instead the Project Manager used the project mandate to produce a simple Project Initiation Documentation (PIO). The PIO includes the Business Case, a product checklist and several Product Descriptions, Including the Project Product Description. Short sections are also included for each of the strategies and the controls to be applied. The Project Manager has elected to use the Daily Log to record all risks, issues, lessons and quality - results.
After the initiation stage there will be two further stages during which a small number of Work Packages will be authorized. While these are being managed, the Project Manager will hold regular checkpoints, which will support the production

of weekly Highlight Reports to the Project Board.

This question provides a number of changes which may or may not be required to the Extract from the Communication Management Strategy provided in the additional information.

Which statement applies to the Introduction section?

A. No change to entry 1 because this shows the purpose and content of this document.
B. Amend entry 1 to read 'This document contains the controls and reporting to be established for the project managementteam'.
C. Amend entry 1 to read 'This document contains the means and frequency of communication between the project management team, the print company and other external parties.

Section: Starting up and Initiating a Project

QUESTION 116
Scenario
Additional Information

Extract from the Communication Management Strategy.
The project information in the table below is true, but it may not be recorded under the correct heading or be in the correct document.

Introduction	1. This document contains details of how the project management team will send information to individuals working on the Calendar project, and receive information from them.
Communication procedure	2. See MNO Manufacturing Company standards for all internal company communications.
Tools and techniques	3. Use the staff newsletter to launch the label design competition and to promote the chosen label design. 4. Using the number of responses to the label design competition as a measure, report fortnightly to the Project Board on the effectiveness of the staff newsletter as a vehicle for communication. 5. Use the company website to advertise the promotional calendar to customers.
Records	6. A record should be maintained for each product of the project. As a minimum this should show the project name, product name, product title, and version number. 7. External email and correspondence relating to the Calendar project should be recorded electronically in the project folder. 8. Information received in hard copy should, where possible, be scanned and filed as above.
Timing of communication activities	9. At the end of each stage, audit and report on the performance of the communication methods being used. 10. Highlight Reports to be provided to appropriate stakeholders, at the frequency defined in each Stage Plan.
Stakeholder analysis: Interested parties	11. Photographer. 12. Print company.
Information needs for each interested party	13. Weekly updates will be provided by email to the individual producing the staff newsletter. 14. Engineering Manager is to be consulted when preparing the photo session schedule.

Using the Project Scenario, select the appropriate response to each of the following 5 questions which have been raised by the Project Board.

The project is now at the end of the initiation stage. Having decided that the Calendar project is a relatively simple project, the Project Manager combined the Starting Up a Project process and the Initiating a Project process. No Project Brief has been produced. Instead the Project Manager used the project mandate to produce a simple Project Initiation Documentation (PIO). The PIO includes the Business Case, a product checklist and several Product Descriptions, Including the Project Product Description. Short sections are also included for each of the strategies and the controls to be applied. The Project Manager has elected to use the Daily Log to record all risks, issues, lessons and quality - results.

After the initiation stage there will be two further stages during which a small number of Work Packages will be authorized. While these are being managed, the Project Manager will hold regular checkpoints, which will support the production of weekly Highlight Reports to the Project Board.

This question provides a number of changes which may or may not be required to the Extract from the Communication Management Strategy provided in the additional information.

Which statement applies to the Tools and techniques section?

A. Delete entry 3 because the activities required to create the products should be documented in the relevant plan(s).

B. Move entry 4 to Reporting because this describes a report on the performance of the Communication procedures used.

C. Delete entry 5 because the customers are not within the scope of this project.

Section: Starting up and Initiating a Project

QUESTION 117
Scenario
Additional Information

Extract from the Communication Management Strategy.
The project information in the table below is true, but it may not be recorded under the correct heading or be in the correct document.

Introduction	1. This document contains details of how the project management team will send information to individuals working on the Calendar project, and receive information from them.
Communication procedure	2. See MNO Manufacturing Company standards for all internal company communications.
Tools and techniques	3. Use the staff newsletter to launch the label design competition and to promote the chosen label design. 4. Using the number of responses to the label design competition as a measure, report fortnightly to the Project Board on the effectiveness of the staff newsletter as a vehicle for communication. 5. Use the company website to advertise the promotional calendar to customers.
Records	6. A record should be maintained for each product of the project. As a minimum this should show the project name, product name, product title, and version number. 7. External email and correspondence relating to the Calendar project should be recorded electronically in the project folder. 8. Information received in hard copy should, where possible, be scanned and filed as above.
Timing of communication activities	9. At the end of each stage, audit and report on the performance of the communication methods being used. 10. Highlight Reports to be provided to appropriate stakeholders, at the frequency defined in each Stage Plan.
Stakeholder analysis: Interested parties	11. Photographer. 12. Print company.
Information needs for each interested party	13. Weekly updates will be provided by email to the individual producing the staff newsletter. 14. Engineering Manager is to be consulted when preparing the photo session schedule.

Using the Project Scenario, select the appropriate response to each of the following 5 questions which have been raised by the Project Board.

The project is now at the end of the initiation stage. Having decided that the

Calendar project is a relatively simple project, the Project Manager combined the Starting Up a Project process and the Initiating a Project process. No Project Brief has been produced. Instead the Project Manager used the project mandate to produce a simple Project Initiation Documentation (PID). The PID includes the Business Case, a product checklist and several Product Descriptions, Including the Project Product Description. Short sections are also included for each of the strategies and the controls to be applied. The Project Manager has elected to use the Daily Log to record all risks, issues, lessons and quality - results.

After the initiation stage there will be two further stages during which a small number of Work Packages will be authorized. While these are being managed, the Project Manager will hold regular checkpoints, which will support the production of weekly Highlight Reports to the Project Board.

This question provides a number of changes which may or may not be required to the Extract from the Communication Management Strategy provided in the additional information.

What statement applies to the Records section?

A. Move entry 6 to the Configuration Management Strategy because it defines the identification scheme for the project's products.
B. Move entry 7 to Communication procedure because it refers to the method to be used for communication to external parties.
C. Move entry 8 to Tools and techniques because it refers to a filing technique.

Section: Starting up and Initiating a Project

QUESTION 118
Scenario
Additional Information

Extract from the Communication Management Strategy.
The project information in the table below is true, but it may not be recorded under the correct heading or be in the correct document.

Introduction	1. This document contains details of how the project management team will send information to individuals working on the Calendar project, and receive information from them.
Communication procedure	2. See MNO Manufacturing Company standards for all internal company communications.
Tools and techniques	3. Use the staff newsletter to launch the label design competition and to promote the chosen label design. 4. Using the number of responses to the label design competition as a measure, report fortnightly to the Project Board on the effectiveness of the staff newsletter as a vehicle for communication. 5. Use the company website to advertise the promotional calendar to customers.
Records	6. A record should be maintained for each product of the project. As a minimum this should show the project name, product name, product title, and version number. 7. External email and correspondence relating to the Calendar project should be recorded electronically in the project folder. 8. Information received in hard copy should, where possible, should be scanned and filed as above.
Timing of communication activities	9. At the end of each stage, audit and report on the performance of the communication methods being used. 10. Highlight Reports to be provided to appropriate stakeholders, at the frequency defined in each Stage Plan.
Stakeholder analysis: Interested parties	11. Photographer. 12. Print company.
Information needs for each interested party	13. Weekly updates will be provided by email to the individual producing the staff newsletter. 14. Engineering Manager is to be consulted when preparing the photo session schedule.

Using the Project Scenario, select the appropriate response to each of the following 5 questions which have been raised by the Project Board. The project is now at the end of the initiation stage. Having decided that the Calendar project is a relatively simple project, the Project Manager combined the Starting Up a Project process and the Initiating a Project process. No Project Brief has been produced. Instead the Project Manager used the project mandate to produce a simple Project Initiation Documentation (PID). The PID includes the Business Case, a product checklist and several Product Descriptions, Including the Project Product Description. Short sections are also included for each of the strategies and the controls to be applied. The Project Manager has elected to use the Daily Log to record all risks, issues, lessons and quality - results.

After the initiation stage there will be two further stages during which a small number of Work Packages will be authorized. While these are being managed, the Project Manager will hold regular checkpoints, which will support the production of weekly Highlight Reports to the Project Board.

This question provides a number of changes which may or may not be required to the Extract from the Communication Management Strategy provided in the additional information.

Which statement applies to the Stakeholder analysis: Interested parties section?

A. Add 'Internal Creative Team'.
B. Delete entry 11 because the photographer is internal to the project management team.
C. Delete entry 12 because the printing of the calendars is outside of the scope

Section: Starting up and Initiating a Project

QUESTION 119
Which statement is an appropriate entry for the project approach heading within the Project Brief?

A. The initial estimates from the feasibility study will be verified during the initiation stage.
B. MFH must better manage suppliers' performance.
C. The Information Technology Division and the Facilities Division will be outsourced to a single service provider.
D. The Project Manager will be responsible for ensuring that the agreed project approach remains an appropriate choice.

Section: Starting up and Initiating a Project

QUESTION 120
While capturing previous lessons, the Project Manager discovered several

interesting facts about outsourcing. Which fact is an appropriate lesson for the

Outsourcing project?

A. Outsourcing is a growth industry and is being implemented by many private sector organizations.
B. Four other government departments are also considering outsourcing some of their business functions next year.
C. Contracts with service providers should include the timescale within which readiness for service is expected following the transfer of equipment and staff.

Section: Starting up and Initiating a Project

QUESTION 121
While planning the initiation stage, the Project Manager reviewed some threats

that had been recorded in the Daily Log. Which threat should have been assessed

for possible risk responses to be included in the Initiation Stage Plan?

A. MFH has no experience in outsourcing and this may affect understanding of what is required, resulting in inadequate plans and strategies.
B. The Project Brief is a complex document and may not be approved by the Executive.
C. There is a shortage of service providers so there is a possibility that no suitable service providers respond to the request for proposals. This would prevent the Outsourcing project from proceeding.

Section: Starting up and Initiating a Project

QUESTION 122

While preparing the Quality Management Strategy, the Project Manager noticed that the corporate quality management system does not specifically cover project management.

Which option provides an appropriate way for the Project Manager proceed?

A. Record the development of a corporate quality management system for project management as a prerequisite of the Project Plan.
B. Proceed with the project without a Quality Management Strategy and adopt the selected service provider's standards in stage 4.
C. Seek relevant organizational standards, then facilitate a workshop to discuss the Quality Management Strategy with Project Assurance.

Section: Starting up and Initiating a Project

QUESTION 123

Which project controls should be established for the Outsourcing project?

A. Highlight Reports to the Project Manager; Exception Reports to the Project Board when project tolerances are forecast to be exceeded.
B. Highlight Reports to the Project Board; Exception Reports to corporate management when stage tolerances are forecast to be exceeded.
C. Highlight Reports to the Project Board; Exception Reports to the Project Board when stage or project tolerances are forecast to be exceeded.

Section: Starting up and Initiating a Project

QUESTION 124

Project Scenario – Health and Safety Training Project:

ABC Company is a well-established training company that uses a standard model to develop training materials and deliver courses to customers.

ABC Company has commissioned a project in response to recent changes in government legislation relating to health and safety on construction sites. The project will deliver "capability to provide health and safety training", including the materials needed for classroom-based training and e-learning. The expected benefits for construction companies include a reduction in lost days and legal costs due to accidents.

The e-learning course will be developed by a specialist external consultancy. The materials for classroom-based training will be delivered by ABC Company's development team. All course materials will be piloted before they are used. ABC Company will deliver training to its customers and also hopes to sell the course materials to other training companies as part of their operational business. ABC Company will use their own sales and marketing departments to promote the courses.

The legislation requires construction companies to comply with the new legislation within two years. The course materials and trainers have to be accredited by a government agency before courses can be delivered. ABC Company is planning to deliver pilot courses within five months of starting the project.

The ABC Company standard development model for new courses recommends the following stages:

End of the Project scenario.

Additional Information:

The Chief Executive Officer (CEO) founded the company five years ago. Under her leadership, ABC Company has grown quickly into a successful training company. It delivers a range of accredited professional training.

The Finance Director is also a founder member of ABC Company and is responsible for authorizing budgets for the Operations and Development Teams. She authorizes all large contracts personally.

The Purchasing Manager reports to the Finance Director and is responsible for managing and monitoring supplier contracts.

The Operations Director is responsible for the delivery off all training and for the training development budget. His department organizes courses, venues and trainers. They work with the Product and the Sales teams to provide a comprehensive training schedule. ABC Company's IT manager reports to the Operations Director.

The <u>Business Development Director</u> has recently been appointed to identify new training needs and propose new products. She will work with the Operations. Director to ensure a cost-conscious approach and that appropriate development technologies are used for the health and safety course.

The <u>Training Development Manager</u> reports to the Business Development Director and is responsible for developing training materials and gaining accreditation, in accordance with the standard course development model. Course developers in his team have skills in a range of development technologies and are allocated to projects as needed.

The <u>Training Delivery Manager</u>, who reports to the Operations Director, is responsible for ensuring that internal and external trainers deliver ABC Company training courses to the required standard. He also checks course materials to ensure they are fit for purpose and of the required quality.

The <u>Central Services Director</u> has responsibility for corporate communications, facilities management and configuration management. He recently led a project to consolidate all company quality systems into one quality management system and set up a corporate quality department, now managed by the Corporate Quality Manager.

The <u>Corporate Document Manager</u> reports to the Central Services Director. She helped establish the company's document management system and now operates

it across the business. She manages a team of administrators and contracts staff when workload is high.

The <u>Sales Director</u> joined ABC Company two months ago and is keen to establish himself by suggesting new markets for the courses and material. All account managers and the marketing team report to him. They promote existing training courses to other training companies and existing customers.
End of the additional information.

ABC Company has decided to include the Health and Safety Training Project in a programme to support their strategy to deliver globally. The programme team has provided the detailed business justification and, as a result, the project board has decided that the business case will not need refining further during the 'initiating a project' process.
Is this an appropriate action for the project board, and why?

A. Yes, because the project board are able to use the business case provided by the programme.
B. Yes, because when the project is part of a programme, the programme team provides the business case.
C. No, because the programme team cannot constrain the project manager's choices.
D. No, because each project in the programme will need a revised business case.

Section: Starting up and Initiating a Project

QUESTION 125
When does Directing a Project begin?

A. From the beginning of Starting up a Project
B. From the beginning of Initiating a Project
C. From the completion of Starting up a Project
D. From the completion of Initiating a Project

Section: Directing a Project, Controlling a Stage and Managing Product Delivery

QUESTION 126

Which of the following is NOT a trigger for the project manager to authorize a work package?

A. Stage Authorization
B. Corrective Action
C. Exception plan approved
D. Reporting highlights

Section: Directing a Project, Controlling a Stage and Managing Product Delivery

QUESTION 127
During a work package the Team manager needs to keep the project manager informed, which management product is used for this?

A. Highlight report
B. Checkpoint Report
C. Issue Report
D. End Stage Report

Section: Directing a Project, Controlling a Stage and Managing Product Delivery

QUESTION 128

While producing the Team Plan to deliver the agreed Work Package, it became apparent that the user representatives assigned 10 check some of the products were unsuitable.

Which 2 actions should the Team Manager take in response to this situation?

A. Consult the Senior Supplier to assign suitable reviewers.
B. Discuss the situation with Project Assurance and agree the changes or additions to the reviewers. Advise the Project Manager of this risk.
C. Ensure the Quality Register is updated with details of the agreed amendments to the reviewers.
D. Notify the Project Manager by raising an Exception Report explaining that the original reviewers are unsuitable.

Section: Directing a Project, Controlling a Stage and Managing Product Delivery

QUESTION 129

Two weeks after starting work the Team Manager noticed that each completed product had exceeded its estimated effort by around 10%. If this trend continues the Work Package will exceed its agreed cost tolerance of 5%.

Which 2 actions should the Team Manager take in response to this situation?

A. Check the status of the products currently being worked on and analyze the effort expended, to determine if the trend is continuing.
B. Update the Team Plan by increasing all future work estimates by 10%.
C. Amend the Work Package and ensure that the revised targets are met.
D. Escalate the situation in the next Checkpoint Report.
E. Raise an issue that costs will exceed tolerance if the current trend continues.

Section: Directing a Project, Controlling a Stage and Managing Product Delivery

QUESTION 130
Project Scenario – Health and Safety Training Project:

ABC Company is a well-established training company that uses a standard model to develop training materials and deliver courses to customers.

ABC Company has commissioned a project in response to recent changes in government legislation relating to health and safety on construction sites. The project will deliver "capability to provide health and safety training", including the materials needed for classroom-based training and e-learning. The expected benefits for construction companies include a reduction in lost days and legal costs due to accidents.

The e-learning course will be developed by a specialist external consultancy. The materials for classroom-based training will be delivered by ABC Company's development team. All course materials will be piloted before they are used. ABC Company will deliver training to its customers and also hopes to sell the course materials to other training companies as part of their operational business. ABC Company will use their own sales and marketing departments to promote the courses.

The legislation requires construction companies to comply with the new legislation within two years. The course materials and trainers have to be accredited by a government agency before courses can be delivered. ABC Company is planning to deliver pilot courses within five months of starting the project.

The ABC Company standard development model for new courses recommends the following stages:

End of the Project scenario.

Additional Information:

The <u>Chief Executive Officer (CEO)</u> founded the company five years ago. Under her leadership, ABC Company has grown quickly into a successful training company. It delivers a range of accredited professional training.

The <u>Finance Director</u> is also a founder member of ABC Company and is responsible for authorizing budgets for the Operations and Development Teams. She authorizes all large contracts personally.

The <u>Purchasing Manager</u> reports to the Finance Director and is responsible for managing and monitoring supplier contracts.

The <u>Operations Director</u> is responsible for the delivery off all training and for the training development budget. His department organizes courses, venues and trainers. They work with the Product and the Sales teams to provide a comprehensive training schedule. ABC Company's IT manager reports to the Operations Director.

The <u>Business Development Director</u> has recently been appointed to identify new training needs and propose new products. She will work with the Operations. Director to ensure a cost-conscious approach and that appropriate development technologies are used for the health and safety course.

The <u>Training Development Manager</u> reports to the Business Development Director and is responsible for developing training materials and gaining accreditation, in accordance with the standard course development model.

Course developers in his team have skills in a range of development technologies and are allocated to projects as needed.

The Training Delivery Manager, who reports to the Operations Director, is responsible for ensuring that internal and external trainers deliver ABC Company training courses to the required standard. He also checks course materials to ensure they are fit for purpose and of the required quality.

The Central Services Director has responsibility for corporate communications, facilities management and configuration management. He recently led a project to consolidate all company quality systems into one quality management system and set up a corporate quality department, now managed by the Corporate Quality Manager.

The Corporate Document Manager reports to the Central Services Director. She helped establish the company's document management system and now operates it across the business. She manages a team of administrators and contracts staff when workload is high.

The Sales Director joined ABC Company two months ago and is keen to establish himself by suggesting new markets for the courses and material. All account managers and the marketing team report to him. They promote existing training courses to other training companies and existing customers.

End of the additional information.

The project is at the start of stage 3, and there will be six teams working on product delivery. In order to exercise control, the project manager has asked each team to submit a detailed team plan for approval. The external team manager for the 'e-learning course' has agreed to submit a summary to the project manager, but will submit the detailed team plan to the senior supplier to review and approve.
Is the team manager's response appropriate, and why?

A. Yes, because a supplier may want to keep the details of the specialist work confidential.
B. Yes, because team plans are mandatory on a project of this size and complexity.
C. No, because the project manager needs detailed plans to manage the work of several teams.
D. No, because the team plan must be submitted to project assurance to check it is viable.

Section: Directing a Project, Controlling a Stage and Managing Product Delivery

QUESTION 131
Project Scenario – Health and Safety Training Project:

ABC Company is a well-established training company that uses a standard model to develop training materials and deliver courses to customers.

ABC Company has commissioned a project in response to recent changes in government legislation relating to health and safety on construction sites. The project will deliver "capability to provide health and safety training", including the materials needed for classroom-based training and e-learning. The expected benefits for construction companies include a reduction in lost days and legal costs due to accidents.

The e-learning course will be developed by a specialist external consultancy. The materials for classroom-based training will be delivered by ABC Company's development team. All course materials will be piloted before they are used. ABC Company will deliver training to its customers and also hopes to sell the course materials to other training companies as part of their operational business. ABC Company will use their own sales and marketing departments to promote the courses.

The legislation requires construction companies to comply with the new legislation within two years. The course materials and trainers have to be accredited by a government agency before courses can be delivered. ABC Company is planning to deliver pilot courses within five months of starting the project.

The ABC Company standard development model for new courses recommends the following stages:

End of the Project scenario.

Additional Information:

The <u>Chief Executive Officer (CEO)</u> founded the company five years ago. Under her leadership, ABC Company has grown quickly into a successful training company. It delivers a range of accredited professional training.

The <u>Finance Director</u> is also a founder member of ABC Company and is responsible for authorizing budgets for the Operations and Development Teams. She authorizes all large contracts personally.

The <u>Purchasing Manager</u> reports to the Finance Director and is responsible for managing and monitoring supplier contracts.

The <u>Operations Director</u> is responsible for the delivery off all training and for the

training development budget. His department organizes courses, venues and trainers. They work with the Product and the Sales teams to provide a comprehensive training schedule. ABC Company's IT manager reports to the Operations Director.

The <u>Business Development Director</u> has recently been appointed to identify new training needs and propose new products. She will work with the Operations. Director to ensure a cost-conscious approach and that appropriate development technologies are used for the health and safety course.

The <u>Training Development Manager</u> reports to the Business Development Director and is responsible for developing training materials and gaining accreditation, in accordance with the standard course development model. Course developers in his team have skills in a range of development technologies and are allocated to projects as needed.

The <u>Training Delivery Manager</u>, who reports to the Operations Director, is responsible for ensuring that internal and external trainers deliver ABC Company training courses to the required standard. He also checks course materials to ensure they are fit for purpose and of the required quality.

The <u>Central Services Director</u> has responsibility for corporate communications, facilities management and configuration management. He recently led a project to consolidate all company quality systems into one quality management system and set up a corporate quality department, now managed by the Corporate Quality Manager.

The <u>Corporate Document Manager</u> reports to the Central Services Director. She helped establish the company's document management system and now operates it across the business. She manages a team of administrators and contracts staff when workload is high.

The <u>Sales Director</u> joined ABC Company two months ago and is keen to establish himself by suggesting new markets for the courses and material. All account managers and the marketing team report to him. They promote existing training courses to other training companies and existing customers.

End of the additional information.

The project is in stage 2. The project manager is reviewing stage status and has collected the checkpoint reports from the team managers. These show that the products are being completed on schedule. However, project support has raised issues that quality reviews have not been completed as agreed. The project manager reports in the highlight report that the stage is progressing well. Is this appropriate, and why?

A. Yes, because the highlight report is a summary of the information in the checkpoint reports.
B. Yes, because the highlight report is used to provide the project board with stage and project progress.
C. No, because the project manager should have recorded the cause of the delay to the quality reviews in the lessons log.
D. No, because the issues raised by project support are a cause for concern and should be reflected in the highlight report.

Section: Directing a Project, Controlling a Stage and Managing Product Delivery

QUESTION 132
Which of the following activities is NOT an action of preparing for planned closure?

A. Update the project plan with actual
B. Update the Project Management Team
C. Request a product status account
D. Confirm project has delivered what is defined in Project Product Description

Section: Managing a Stage Boundary and Closing a Project

QUESTION 133
Which principle is supported by the activity Evaluate the Project?

A. Continued Business Justification
B. Defined roles and responsibilities
C. Learn from experience
D. Manage by stages

Section: Managing a Stage Boundary and Closing a Project

ANSWERS

1. Correct Answer: AE
2. Correct Answer: AC
3. Correct Answer: BD
4. Correct Answer: CD
5. Correct Answer: CD
6. Correct Answer: CD
7. Correct Answer: CD
8. Correct Answer: CD
9. Correct Answer: CE
10. Correct Answer: AB
11. Correct Answer: BD
12. Correct Answer:

	Assertion	True-False	Reason	True-False
1	The selected service provider should have their own Business Case for the work they are doing on the Outsourcing project.	True-False A	All project costs, including the cost of work carried out by external suppliers on the project should be included in the customer's Business Case.	True-False
2	The cost of managing the outsourcing contract should be included in the Business Case.	True-False B	The information in the Business Case is used to compare the development, maintenance and operational costs with the value of the benefits over a period of time.	True-False
3	The Business options section of the Business Case will need to be updated if the industry standards for outsourcing are changed.	True-False C	The Business options section of the Business Case describes options that have been considered to address the business problem.	True-False
4	Any expected benefit from increasing staff flexibility should be included in the Business Case.	True-False D	The Business Case should list each benefit that is claimed would be achieved by the project's outcome.	True-False
5	The End Project Report should identify whether the expected savings of £2 over 10 years have been achieved.	True-False E	All benefits in the Business Case should be achieved before a project is closed.	True-False
6	The Project Board should ensure that the Benefits Review Plan includes the mechanisms for measuring all the claimed benefits of outsourcing.	True-False F	The Benefits Review Plan is created in the initiation stage.	True-False

13. Correct Answer: B
14. Correct Answer: A
15. Correct Answer: B
16. Correct Answer: A
17. Correct Answer: C
18. Correct Answer: CD
19. Correct Answer: DE

20. Correct Answer: AC
21. Correct Answer: CE
22. Correct Answer: AB
23. Correct Answer: BC
24. Correct Answer: AE
25. Correct Answer: BC
26. Correct Answer: BC
27. Correct Answer: AB
28. Correct Answer: DE
29. Correct Answer: BE
30. Correct Answer: D
31. Correct Answer: A
32. Correct Answer: D
33. Correct Answer: A
34. Correct Answer:

	Introduction
	Information relating to the health and safety training courses can be shared with third parties. This is an exception to normal policy.
	Tools and techniques
	Signed non-disclosure agreements should be copied and stored with project documentation.
	A list of the signed non-disclosure agreements will be provided to corporate management on a monthly basis.
	Roles and responsibilities

35. Correct Answer: D
36. Correct Answer: B

37. Correct Answer: B
38. Correct Answer: A
39. Correct Answer: B
40. Correct Answer: C
41. Correct Answer: D
42. Correct Answer:

Column 1	Column 2
Understanding the customer's quality expectations.	Quality planning
Approval of the project's products.	Quality control
Confirmation that corporate management standards and policies are being adhered to.	Quality assurance

43. Correct Answer: AB
44. Correct Answer: CD
45. Correct Answer: DE
46. Correct Answer: BE
47. Correct Answer: AC
48. Correct Answer: A
49. Correct Answer: C
50. Correct Answer: C
51. Correct Answer: D
52. Correct Answer: C
53. Correct Answer: D
54. Correct Answer: A
55. Correct Answer: D
56. Correct Answer: C

57. Correct Answer: C
58. Correct Answer: D
59. Correct Answer: A
60. Correct Answer: D
61. Correct Answer: D
62. Correct Answer: A
63. Correct Answer: B
64. Correct Answer: C
65. Correct Answer: A
66. Correct Answer: AC
67. Correct Answer: AE
68. Correct Answer: AD
69. Correct Answer: A
70. Correct Answer: A
71. Correct Answer: D
72. Correct Answer: A
73. Correct Answer: C
74. Correct Answer: A
75. Correct Answer: C
76. Correct Answer: D
77. Correct Answer: BD
78. Correct Answer: BC
79. Correct Answer: BE
80. Correct Answer: BD
81. Correct Answer: CD
82. Correct Answer: A
83. Correct Answer: B
84. Correct Answer: B
85. Correct Answer: C

86. Correct Answer: D
87. Correct Answer: C
88. Correct Answer: B

89. Correct Answer:

90. Correct Answer: A
91. Correct Answer: C
92. Correct Answer: D
93. Correct Answer: A
94. Correct Answer: A
95. Correct Answer: C

96. Correct Answer: D
97. Correct Answer: A
98. Correct Answer: B
99. Correct Answer: C
100. Correct Answer: B
101. Correct Answer: C
102. Correct Answer: D
103. Correct Answer: DE
104. Correct Answer: DE
105. Correct Answer: AB
106. Correct Answer:

The 'e-learning course' will be accessible by users for 10 hrs each day +/- 2 hrs per day.	The 'e-learning course' will be accessible by users for 10 hrs each day +/- 2 hrs per day.
The 'classroom-based training material' must include slides and exercises. It should also include pre-course reading.	Cost
Company A plans to generate £1000,000 +/- 10%.	Company A plans to generate £1000,000 +/- 10%.
	The 'classroom-based training material' must include slides and exercises. It should also include pre-course reading.
	The 'e-learning course' will be accessible by users for 10 hrs each day +/- 2 hrs per day.

107. Correct Answer: A
108. Correct Answer: D
109. Correct Answer: C
110. Correct Answer: B
111. Correct Answer: C
112. Correct Answer: C
113. Correct Answer: A

114. Correct Answer: C
115. Correct Answer: A
116. Correct Answer: B
117. Correct Answer: A
118. Correct Answer: A
119. Correct Answer: C
120. Correct Answer: C
121. Correct Answer: C
122. Correct Answer: C
123. Correct Answer: C
124. Correct Answer: A
125. Correct Answer: C
126. Correct Answer: D
127. Correct Answer: B
128. Correct Answer: AB
129. Correct Answer: AE
130. Correct Answer: C
131. Correct Answer: D
132. Correct Answer: B
133. Correct Answer: C

www.ingramcontent.com/pod-product-compliance
Lightning Source LLC
Chambersburg PA
CBHW060839220526
45466CB00003B/1168